Communicating Conviction

Communicating Conviction

R. T. BROOKS

EPWORTH PRESS

7162 0393 6

First published 1983
by Epworth Press
Room 195, 1 Central Buildings, Westminster,
London SW1

Typeset by Gloucester Typesetting Services
and printed in Great Britain by
Richard Clay (The Chaucer Press) Ltd
Bungay, Suffolk

Contents

Introduction   vii

1   The Nature of the Task   1

2   Twentieth-Century Influences   15

3   Words   31

4   Stories   47

5   Pictures   67

6   Dialogue   82

7   Theory   98

8   Worship   110

9   A Changing Scene: The Electronic Media   123

    Notes   143

Introduction

The origins of this book need to be explained and that requires a few lines of autobiography, self-indulgent as that may seem.

After working as a minister in a couple of (then) Congregational churches in Yorkshire I joined the BBC's Religious Broadcasting Department. I spent eleven years producing mostly radio programmes in Manchester and then rather more than eighteen years producing television programmes in London. When I reached the BBC's retiring age I felt I should try to use that specialist experience rather than return at once to a local pastorate. In the five years which have now elapsed I have been able to do a certain amount of continuing work in radio and television (and in places where broadcasting skills are taught), but I have also tried to do some more fundamental thinking about the ways in which religious conviction is communicated from one to another, not just in broadcasting but anywhere.

I was lucky in that a number of groups and organizations allowed me to share my thinking with them. In particular I have been able for three successive years to spend one day a week of one term a year with Methodist and Baptist theological students in Bristol. These sessions included practical exercises with audio and video recorders, but always started with what I suppose must be called a lecture. This was because it became increasingly apparent that the strengthening of Christian communication is at least as much a matter of content as of presentation, even more a matter of applied theology than of applied technology. The chapters which follow contain the substance of the most recent version of those introductory talks in Bristol.

I hope they will be of use to a wider constituency. Theological students are not a race apart. Their concern for the communication of Christian faith is widely shared. They are themselves well aware that it cannot be done by the ordained ministry alone, and that it cannot be done just through preaching or writing or radio or television. All believers are involved and every medium of communication is involved – from chatting at a bus stop, through songs and stories to the most solemn affirmations of liturgical worship. Indeed, I would say that to understand better how our faith is communicated is to understand better what our faith is.

So the book is designed for the general reader. My own particular debt, however, is to the department of the BBC which employed me, to the colleges which made time and space for me and to the students who helped me to see something of what is involved in communicating an ancient faith to twentieth-century people.

I

The Nature of the Task

Seven years of silent enquiry are needful for a man to learn the truth, but fourteen in order to learn how to make it known to his fellow men (Plato).

Since Plato lived some four centuries before Christ he can hardly be called a Christian, but the above quotation appears in *The Hodder Book of Christian Quotations* – presumably because it is a good thought for Christians to take account of. In fact it could be said to understate rather than to overstate their problem. Christians are concerned not merely to articulate a truth in such a way that another mind can grasp it, but to impart conviction in such a way that others share it. What is more, communicating this conviction involves drawing people into an experience of the transcendent, and for many today that is a dimension which has no reality. They may or may not believe that there is a God, but often they live with no sense of a divine Presence. They do not stand in awe and wonder before a mystery to which the Christian communicator will give a name and a shape.

The problems are therefore formidable. And those problems cannot be brushed aside by invoking the mysterious power of the Holy Spirit as the only true communicator. In this matter as in others the Holy Spirit uses human agents. They are therefore required to fashion the best possible tools of communication for the Spirit's use. We are told to pray as if it all depended on God and to act as if it all depended on us. So here. And applied to the field of communication this injunction requires us to begin by thinking about the place which communication occupies in human experience generally.

Computers may pass data from one memory bank to another. That is not human communication. Among humans significant communication is deeply related to the experience of personhood and to the experience of inter-personal relationships. John Macquarrie confirms this.

> Communication . . . is not to be thought of as the transferring of ideas from one thinking subject to another. That might be propaganda or suggestion, but it would not be genuine communication, for this involves a sharing . . . Communication takes place when some aspect of the shared world is lit up and made accessible to both parties in the discourse . . . all communication is interpretation.[1]

John Macquarrie is, of course, a Christian theologian and his understanding of communication is deeply biblical. In fact the entire biblical story can be read as an account of the making, the breaking and the restoring of communication. It starts with the affirmation that the universe is created by God's word. The tangible creation is an utterance, an expression of God's mind. The world *is* communication.

Moreover, humanity is created for and by inter-personal communication. It is significant that in Genesis' symbolic story Adam is no sooner created than God speaks to him. And 'Adam', I understand, is not a term which distinguishes a male from a female: it is humanity as such which is designed for communication with God. But humanity is also designed for communication within itself. In chapter two of Genesis humanity is divided into man and woman precisely in order that the individual will not be alone. Adam has named the animals (and that would seem to imply an intention to talk about them as well as symbolizing authority over them), but there is still need for a partner capable of dialogue. 'It is not good that the man should be alone.' Hence man and woman. Communication one with another is essential to being human as the Bible portrays humanity. The idyllic picture in Genesis is possibly more useful as a symbol of the human goal rather than of human origins. This is the true humanity to which we are called. Our actual condition is more accurately conveyed by the pictures which follow the Genesis account of the fall.

First comes the breaking of man's power to communicate with God. An angel with a turning sword bars the way of open access to the divine presence. Then comes the breaking of man's power to communicate with other men. From Babel humanity is scattered into groups no longer capable of understanding each other. The effects of human arrogance are pictured as primarily a breakdown of communication.

Neither within humanity nor between humanity and God is the breakdown said to be total. Some inter-human communication is still possible and some communication between humanity and God as well. To some extent mankind – *all* mankind (see Gen. 9.6) – retains the characteristic of being made in God's image. To some extent God still communicates with people – typically through the prophets. To some extent people still communicate with God – typically in the Psalms. But the messages are confused and distorted. Even when clearly delivered, there is a tendency in people to reject God's communications in favour of something better suited to human convenience and pride.

There is a dramatic example of this in the story told both in I Kings 22 and in II Chronicles 18. It tells of the time when Israel was divided into two kingdoms. Jehoshaphat, ruler of the southern kingdom, visits Samaria for a meeting with the northern king, Ahab. According to Chronicles the visiting king was welcomed with a great feast. In that case Jehoshaphat was one of the first to learn the truth of a much more recent dictum: 'there is no such thing as a free lunch'. Before the meal has ended Ahab is proposing a joint expedition to recover Ramoth-gilead from the Syrians. Jehoshaphat is all politeness: 'I am as you are, my people as your people. We will be with you in the war.' However, he knows how to use piety as an instrument of policy – and of prevarication. He adds, 'Inquire first for the word of the Lord.'

Ahab is ready for such religiosity. He has a team of four hundred prophets who can quickly be called in and can also be relied upon to say what suits their king. Asked whether or not an attack should be launched against Ramoth-gilead they answer as one: 'Go up; for God will give it into the hand of the king.'

Jehoshaphat remains unsatisfied. 'Is there not here another prophet of the Lord of whom we may inquire?'

Four hundred prophets he has already and he wants another one! Of course he does. The four hundred are not saying what he wants to hear. Naturally he finds them unconvincing. But it soon emerges that Ahab has been acting on just the same principle of selectivity. 'There is yet one man by whom we may inquire of the Lord, Micaiah the son of Imlah; but I hate him, for he never prophesies good concerning me, but always evil.' Who can hear the unpalatable word?

While the four hundred continue prophesying success – and doing it with increasing frenzy and dramatic symbolism – a messenger is sent. The messenger is himself one of those who wants prophecy filtered through some kind of grid which will strain out the inconvenient truth. He says to Micaiah, 'Behold, the words of the prophets with one accord are favourable to the king; let your word be like the word of one of them, and speak favourably.' It is left to Micaiah to say, 'As the Lord lives, what my God says, that I will speak.'

Eventually he did. And equally naturally he was disregarded. Only when hard experience had proved him to be right was his word accepted as truly prophetic. Present-day parallels are not hard to find. We live by communication, but we have a bias towards distortion and only experience can cure it.

But the New Testament has as one of its central themes the possibility of restoring open communication with God and between people. The first chapter of John reads like a restatement of the first chapter of Genesis. The light of the creative Word has been encompassed by darkness, but the darkness has not extinguished it and now the Word has become flesh and dwelt among us. The opening of Hebrews repeats the story in terms equally concerned with communication: 'In many and various ways God spoke of old to our fathers by the prophets; but in these last days he has spoken to us by a Son, whom he appointed the heir of all things, through whom also he created the world.'

Both passages speak of restored communication, and when Luke comes to tell the story of Pentecost it is almost as if he has deliberately reversed the story of Babel. The language barrier which had divided humanity ceases to be effective. Under the power of the Spirit each hears the message in his own tongue. The story is not told as an experience of speaking in tongues – though that may have been what actually happened – but as a symbolic healing of the wounds of Babel. The message has broken through the barriers of culture.

What is more, man's capacity for communication with God is restored too. According to Paul it is still done with groaning and wrestling, but the Spirit within him moves him to say 'Abba, Father', and teaches him what needs to be said.

So the centrality of communication to the nature of man and to the story of his redemption is massively affirmed. Indeed, it is derived not merely from the nature of man but from the nature of God. John V. Taylor, Bishop of Winchester, regards all true communication as a sort of participation in the life of the Trinity.

> Every time I am given this unexpected awareness towards some other creature and feel this current of communication between us, I am touched and activated by something that comes from the fiery heart of the divine love, the eternal gaze of the Father towards the Son, of the Son towards the Father.[2]

Even the modern emphasis on *techniques* of communication is not all that exclusively modern. I understand that the *trivium*, the three early stages of a mediaeval education, consisted of grammar, rhetoric and logic. G. S. Fraser explains the purpose of such a training.

> Grammar taught you how to express yourself correctly, rhetoric how to express yourself effectively, logic . . . how to be sure that you are not correctly and effectively talking self-contradictory nonsense.[3]

That sounds to me just like a course on communication – and one with a very proper emphasis on the need to think about form and content as parts of a single whole. It does not allow methods and techniques of communication to be mere packaging designed to give a spurious appearance of appealing rationality regardless of the actual content.

Two things *are* perhaps distinctive about the modern interest in communication. One is the emphasis on the very personal nature of significant communication – the sort of emphasis to be found in the above quotations from John Macquarrie and John V. Taylor. Perhaps our experience of impersonal, computerized exchanges of information has alerted us to the distinctively personal character of truly human communication. Perhaps we have also been alarmed by mass communication techniques capable of trampling on an individual personality or a local culture.

If one present-day emphasis is on the personal, the other is naturally on the variety of media available and on the influence these have on both the form and the content of effective communication. I would argue that there are in fact three elements which have to be brought into harmony with one another before communication can flow in such a way as to fulfil the Christian understanding of communication as communion, as fellowship. They are the content of the communication; the recipient of the communication; the medium through which the message reaches the recipient. Each of these three has to be appropriate to the other two. However true the message, if it is not presented in a form appropriate to the medium and to the recipient it cannot communicate conviction. However close a communicator may get to those with whom he (including she) is communicating, if he forgets the relevant truth of his faith or embodies it in a message inappropriate to his medium, no conviction will be communicated. However expert a communicator may be in the skills of a particular medium, if the message is defective or does not fit the needs of the recipient, the communication of conviction will not take place.

The matching of these three elements will be the predominant concern of the rest of this book, but it is necessary to give a little attention to each separately by way of introduction.

The medium

By 'the medium' I do not just mean one of 'the media' in the modern sense. I use the term to cover both the signalling system that is used and the whole context of events around it. So speech is a different medium in different situations, and there are many other media. Body language is a medium of communication just as much as broadcasting or writing in a newspaper. Each has its own context and imposes its own requirements. Chatting over a garden fence requires a communication different in form and content from those of a sermon just because it is a different medium. The sermon requires a form and content different from those of broadcasting because it is a different medium. And so on.

I am not saying that the medium should be allowed to dominate. I sometimes tell a cautionary tale about an imaginary (but not all *that* imaginary) American evangelist. He felt that he was reaching too few people, so he went to the experts for advice. In New York he talked to an advertising agency or a public relations specialist and said something like this.

'I have a message. I believe it's a great message. But not enough people are listening to it. Can you help me present my message in such a way that it will reach a bigger audience?'

'We'd love to,' said the experts. 'We like your message and we can see what's lacking in your presentation. Put yourself in our hands and we'll deliver you an audience many times larger than you have ever known. But this is the age of television. You'll need a really professional television programme as your vehicle. Here is the address of a company that can really deliver the goods. And we'll promote the finished product.'

So my imaginary evangelist made the long journey from East to West to see a television production company in Hollywood. He put much the same questions and received much the same reply. 'Sure. We'd love to. We know how to pull an audience. We'll have them waiting for your message with their eyes and their ears (and their cheque books) all wide open.'

So everybody went to work with a will, not realizing that they had already made their big mistake. They had assumed that presentation and content are separable, that medium and message can be conceived independently. If the product were soap, maybe they could. If you package soap brightly enough and then promote it with all the right images, it is possible that people will buy the product for the packaging and the self-image associated with it. That could be all right because what comes out of the package is still soap. You actually can wash with it. But if the product is an idea and you wrap it up in a more appealing idea, who is to say that the package will ever be opened and the true contents put to use?

However, my imaginary preacher now has what he bargained for. He is the star of a popular television programme. A typical edition starts with two small children toddling on hand in hand. One of them lisps the script-writer's introduction to the programme – a shrewd mixture of the winsome and the pious. The audience in the studio/church responds warmly so that the viewing audience will be encouraged to do the same.

Next comes the choir. A number of very pretty girls and matching boys are deployed in well-staged groups over a considerable area. (They would hardly be able to sing in such positions, but that does not matter because the sound is pre-recorded.) The lyrics they sing are impeccably religious – jingles maybe, but *religious* jingles. The tunes are easy on the ear and richly harmonized. Nothing discordant appears in sound or vision.

Then the preacher is announced – with declamation – and comes on to deliver his message. But does he really need to? The message of the programme has already been delivered not by its content but by its form. Its message as expressed by the glossy presentation is a promise of success, the fulfilment of the American dream, stardom, a life of comfort and harmony. The brave preacher may speak about starvation in the South or war in the East, he may even quote so discordant a text as 'Take up your cross and follow me', but the medium within which he is working does not allow such a call to penetrate. It is all absorbed into the reassuring warmth of the format. The visual message in particular – and that includes everything from the lighting to the preacher's suit – can block the verbal one.

This cautionary tale may be grossly unfair to every actual preacher in the electric church, but it is a healthy warning against failing to subject the form and medium of the message to the same theological scrutiny as its content. In a very real way the style in which the message is presented *is* its content. For a great many recipients of the message *how* it is expressed communicates more than *what* is expressed, so if there is a mismatch between the medium and the message, the medium may prevail.

8

And such things happen, of course, not only in America and not only on the small screen. If the lugubrious tones of a solemn preacher are at variance with his words, the words will have difficulty in prevailing over the tone. If the strident sounds of another are at variance with the humility of the message, the triumphalist tone could well be dominant at the receiving end. Chirpy methods of presentation may communicate a cheerful indifference to suffering even when the whole intention is to express nothing but compassion. The medium – which includes the language style and the vocal tone as well as its technical form – needs to be adjusted to the message and to the recipient of the message. It must be theologically and psychologically disciplined. It is never (to throw a variety of analogies into one pot) just a sales technique, just a wrapping, just sugar on a pill, just a sprat to catch a mackerel. It is always itself communicating a message.

The message

This time not the message accidentally communicated, but the *intended* message, the real content of the communication. The message in this sense must be supreme, and yet it must be humble enough to match the medium and the recipient.

There is a religious broadcasting organization on the continent of Europe which makes a point of presenting its messages in what it regards as an uncompromising way. It makes no attempt to win the audience, other than with the solid meat of the Gospel. I have heard the method justified by saying that it is like that of the door-to-door salesman who goes up and down the street repeating the same spiel on every doorstep. Some will buy and some will not. That is their decision and not the salesman's problem. His job is to say it over and over again so that everybody has the chance to respond.

In the same way, it is argued, the religious broadcaster must just say what the Word of God compels him to say and leave the Holy Spirit to make the message effective where He will. Actually, however, this is not quite the way in which the door-to-door salesman works. He does not in fact deliver his spiel until he has rung the bell and got someone to open the door. Broadcasters working to this uncompromising pattern, sincerely convinced as they are, often seem to me to have omitted that stage. They have not directed themselves to the interests and the needs of their hearers, and they have not matched the message to the medium. They have not rung the doorbell, so very few have opened and very few are listening.

Again, I am not saying that the message should be *subject* to the medium. Richard Holloway issues a very severe and proper warning against that.

> Today's theologians are so intent on translating the message into a medium of communication which the world will under-stand that they have allowed the language to replace the reality it was meant to convey. The medium has usurped the message, the style has replaced the substance ... The modern public relations industry has created a situation in which image has become more important than substance, the sell more important than the thing sold. By the time he has captured the public's ear, the jet-age theologian has nothing left to say to them that they don't already know.[4]

That is a healthy warning. As far as Christians are concerned, the message is given. There is no question of our inventing a fresh one to suit the appetites of our time or of our media. But from the riches of that message it is necessary to select that aspect of its truth which is relevant to a particular recipient on a particular occasion. And the nature of the occasion is often determined by the medium which connects the message giver to the message receiver. Neither the medium nor the listener can dictate what Christianity *is*, but they have a right to be offered it in forms which match up to both. The apostle Paul was no trimmer, but he was ready to become all things to all men in order to save some of them.

The recipient of the message

Matching the message and the medium to this third factor demands a lot of human understanding combined with some knowledge of the psychological and sociological factors which condition human responses. How successfully it is being done at the moment is open to doubt. On bad days I am inclined to say that there is nothing much wrong with the churches' communications to those outside their ranks – except merely that we are answering questions which have not been asked, we are doing it in a language which is not understood, and doing it in places where nobody is listening anyway. Otherwise everything is fine!

No doubt the real situation is a good deal better than that, but we still have something to learn about all those three areas.

First, we have something to learn about the questions which are really being asked – not just those which are being articulated in religious debate, but those which are being set by life itself. We need to see into the images which are screened on the back of people's minds and which shape their actions and reactions, we need to speak to their felt needs in such a way as to reach through them to deeper needs than ever they have been aware of.

Even answering the questions actually articulated (as distinct from those we would like to be asked) can be inconvenient. I once had the experience of broadcasting a short weekly answer to listeners' questions on what the Bible had to say about subjects which concerned them. The series started well before Christmas and ran up to Holy Week, so I looked forward to being questioned about the meaning of those festivals. That would be my cue to say my piece about the biblical doctrines of incarnation and atonement. Only *nobody* would write in with the questions I wanted. Incarnation and atonement were very relevant to many of the questions asked repeatedly, but people just would not raise the issues in the form for which I had pre-packaged answers. So the pre-packaged answers never had an airing. I had to try and unfold the significance of incarnation and atonement as a response to practical questions about life in the body and about the cost of reconciliation.[5]

Next, we also have something to learn about the language in which we can be understood. It is not just a matter of avoiding or defining technical terms. It has much more to do with finding the images, the metaphors, the stories which have resonance in our time. Only in such terms can we reach deep into the hearts and minds of our generation. And this is not necessarily the language we habitually use. In fact we sometimes seem deliberately to cultivate a quite different terminology.

In his *Introduction to a Theological Theory of Language* Gerhard Ebeling said that

> ... individual social groups express their distinctive nature in certain forms of speech, and so protect it. That is, they enhance the feeling of union and concord within the group itself by the use of a language with which the outsider is not immediately familiar, and which makes him emphatically aware of the fact that he does not belong.[6]

Some say that young people have for years been inventing a language of their own precisely in order *not* to be understood by their elders. Religious groups are not incapable of developing an in-group language of this kind in order to enhance their cosy sense of togetherness in relation to each other and apartness in relation to everybody else. They can even make converts this way because there are people happy to surrender to any formula which offers an escape from isolation. However, the language of the closed circle can never really speak to the needs of the world at large – only offer a way of evading them.

It has to be said again that speaking in a language the world finds intelligible is pointless if we are only going to say what the world already knows. The familiar words have to be used in unfamiliar ways and made to perform as the unexpected bearers of a new idea. Gerhard Ebeling is himself clear about that.

> A precondition of all knowledge is the shock which is caused by what is not understood, the terror at something strange which provokes questions and thereby initiates the decisive moment in the process of understanding.[7]

But such shocks can only be administered by those who have met in a shared medium and who stand upon some common ground.

That is the third area about which we have much to learn: finding the open channels through which transforming communications can flow. John Macquarrie has already warned us that all communication is the interpretation of shared experience. Finding the right means by which to communicate a message is not just a matter of deciding whether to write it, speak it or broadcast it. It is at least as much a matter of locating the shared experience which can provide common ground for the meeting and an appropriate medium for the message. Of course, the interpretation of that experience will extend the hearer's under-standing of it. It will enrich the familiar words used to describe that experience. It will move the hearer on to experiences previ-ously unknown, but the whole process begins on common ground described in a shared language.

I once had the privilege of introducing and concluding a tele-vision programme in which Mrs Dehqani-Tafti, wife of the Anglican Bishop in Iran, expounded the idea of trust. She started by talking about trust as she had known it in her relations with her children: the trust which her daughter had to show when her mother was in a swimming pool and called on the little girl to jump in and learn to swim, the trust which the mother had to show when an older girl was of an age to be allowed down a busy street on her own. All this must have been common ground with most viewers. They had shared such experiences. They understood the word 'trust' in this sense.

But Mrs Dehqani-Tafti went on from there to talk about what the word meant on the night when Iranian extremists broke into their home and tried to shoot her husband as he lay beside her in bed. She did not mention it, but I believe she threw herself across him and took one of the bullets herself. What she did speak of was her conviction that her husband was so protected by the power of prayer that he could not be hurt. That was what 'trust' meant then, and it seemed in the event to be justified. The Bishop was untouched. But that was not the end.

What came next was an account of what trust meant some months later when the terrorists attacked not her husband but their son, and killed him. 'I was faced with one member of my family having been saved by a trusted God and one being allowed to die.' By this time she was interpreting experiences which none of her viewers would have had, but she was leading them deeper into the shared experience which had provided the original meet-ing point. Both language and life were extended and enriched by her account.

So in the following chapters, although it may be necessary to concentrate for a time on medium, or on message, or on the recipient of the message, the concern will always be to match whichever it is with the other two. And we will start by taking a closer look at the peculiarly twentieth-century characteristics of the recipient.

2

Twentieth-Century Influences

Under the skin the men and women of the twentieth century are sure to be kin to the men and women of all previous centuries. There is the same hankering after the good and inclination to the bad. Human beings are still 'the glory and scum of the universe', still sinners called to be saints.

But all that is under the skin. To communicate with the person under the skin you have to approach from outside it, and the signals you deliver to ear and eye have to pass through a mind which filters and interprets them for itself. In this respect the men and women of the twentieth century do seem to have special features of their own. The filtering and interpreting mechanism through which messages must pass has been conditioned by a variety of factors which are new, and the result is that many messages which get as far as the skin can get no farther – or not without being so distorted as to become unacceptable at the receiving end and to bear little resemblance to what was intended at the transmitting end.

Two features of our time seem to me particularly relevant to those who are trying to communicate religious conviction. One is that many of our present-day assumptions are those of the 'information age', and another is that many of our governing images are those projected into our minds by the media. The Christian communicator who takes no account of these factors may say that he feels he is talking to deaf ears, but what is really happening is more like talking through an interpreter who mistranslates everything that is said.

The information age

I have remembered for quite some years now the experience of walking down a street in London's West End and seeing in the window of a commercial training school the announcement of a course on 'English for Computers'. Should I enroll myself or merely send along my pocket calculator? What was this language, anyway?

I suppose that it was the language we must learn not in order to talk *about* computers but to talk *to* them. Talking *about* computers involves technical terminology as any specialism does, but talking *to* computers – communicating with them, putting sensible questions to them, getting useful answers from them – involves human beings in thinking in a particular way. They need to be data minded. They need to frame and express their ideas with precision, without ambiguity. 'English for Computers' has to be a language of the objective, definitive kind – univocal rather than metaphorical. Try feeding poetic imagery into a computer and you will prove the validity of its basic law: garbage in, garbage out.

As a way of thinking and speaking this habit of mind spreads rapidly far beyond the ranks of those who actually work at data collection and transmission. Indeed, this way of using language has been increasingly dominant ever since the days of Newton and Bacon. It could be said to have produced the computer rather than to have been produced by it. But the more we use such devices (as we surely must), the more readily we assume that this is *the* way of stating and communicating truth. In addition we assume that the statements we receive should be accepted in the same way as literal and definitive statements of hard fact.

Science fiction has frequently played with the idea of computers acquiring human characteristics. A much likelier and more alarming scenario concerns the likelihood of human beings acquiring the characteristics of computers. Already a distinguished professor in the computer section of the Massachusetts Institute of Technology has been heard to complain that we are now only asking the sort of questions which computers can handle. The subtler and more human questions are not taken seriously.

Most of us are still incompetent where computers are concerned (and none the better for that), but we do often adopt the assumption that a statement is either objectively, univocally true or else it is unreliable and useless. Only talking unadorned fact is thought to be talking seriously. To treat facts as signifying anything outside themselves, to treat them as symbolic or sacramental, is an attitude for which the twentieth-century characteristics of the human mind have not prepared us. Today the noun 'symbol' seems to be haunted by the adjective 'mere': symbols are *mere* symbols. 'If the affirmations of the creed are only *symbolically* true,' people say, 'then they're just fancy. So now tell us the *real* truth.'

Equally characteristically, 'Is it true?' applied to a story would mean 'Did it happen just like that? Is the story a piece of accurate reporting? Would a video recording made at the time have given us just these words and actions when played back?' Anyone who has discussed the Epiphany story with young people who are typical of our time is likely to have been asked whether the star was a UFO, whether the child was an extra-terrestial, whether astronomical or astrological calculations offer any clues as to what *really* happened. Images and symbols will be brushed aside in the pursuit of objective explanation. Factuality rather than truth in any larger sense is what the mind is focussed on.

The problems thus set to the religious communicator will be discussed later, but there is also a backlash effect of which we must take account. Man does not live by data alone. So to compensate our minds for their preoccupation with the world of known fact we give them generous holidays in the world of fantasy. Stories which ask to be taken seriously are submitted to the test of factual accuracy and no other, but stories which make no such claim can be as romantic as you please. Minds bruised by their constant butting into cold, hard statements can relax in the world of fantasy.

This seems to apply even to those for whom the objective world has God as its dominant reality. After spending some months working very happily in an American community of conservative evangelicals I began to think that there might be a connection between their biblical literalism and their intense appreciation of C. S. Lewis's *Chronicles of Narnia*. Perhaps their insistence on the historical accuracy of the Bible stories and on the objective truth of its language had left them suffering from a kind of myth starvation – a longing for symbols of transcendence, a hunger for words and images which reflect more than they contain, an appetite which could be appeased in the magical country of Lewis's devout imagination but not in the language of their faith.

Read the Bible as if it had been written by Isaac Newton, and your soul will cry out for something more mysteriously significant. (Though, incidentally, Newton himself perfectly well understood the difference between his way of using words and that of the Old Testament. In his writings on the prophets he made it clear that we cannot begin to understand them until we have grasped their particular way of using imagery.) Religion itself can be understood in terms set by the information age instead of on its own terms. It then becomes both dry and dubious.

Among those from whom the whole idea of God or of heaven is absent, the need for escape from the unpoetic world must be strong indeed. Many people seem to spend more time in the world of fantasy than they do in the world of fact. Their assumption remains: there is a real world which is all data of no symbolic or transcendent significance; there is a fantasy world which is of no practical significance. And that assumption is wrong on both counts. First, Christians will affirm that the real world is a world of sacramental facts, simultaneously objective and symbolic, a tangible mirror of the eternal. Second, the fantasy world is not a world apart where our imaginations can be indulged with no significant consequences: much of our actual living in the concrete world of facts is the product of our fantasies. From the image springs the action.

Controlling images

This brings us to the consideration of the twentieth century's dominant images and of television as one of the important means of implanting them – often without either the implanters or the recipients being aware of what is happening.

Not long ago a local Marriage Guidance Council put together a questionnaire for use by fifth and sixth forms – and by some older people whose answers were to be compared with those of the teenagers. The questions were divided into two main groups. One set asked what features were thought to be most important in the making of a good personal relationship. The other set asked from what sources these ideas had been derived. In the latter category people were asked to assess the influence on them of fiction, of films, of television. One after another of the young people (unlike a clinical psychologist among the older ones!) declared that these had played no part at all in the shaping of their ideas.

This was a surprise to some who knew them. Both boys and girls looked, spoke and behaved very much in the style of the people they read about in stories, saw in advertisements, watched on television, put into the pop charts. Was it really true that none of that helped to mould their attitudes to one another? In one sense, no it was not really true. But neither, I suspect, were the young people lying. What they meant by their answers was that they had not adopted as their own conscious code any principles enunciated for them on television or by characters they read about. They were answering the questions correctly as far as their ideas were concerned, but they were not answering about the images at the back of their minds because they had not considered them. They should. After all, in the world of personal relationships the romantic picture of an ideal relationship could well have more practical effect than a code of conduct held in the head.

And it is not only teenagers who spend their time trying to give reality to an image held in the imagination rather than to a precept adopted in the mind. I remember being told by the editor of the problem page in a popular women's magazine why she was receiving a stream of letters from women who believed themselves to be failures – and whose distress was perfectly real, whatever you may think of their turning to an agony column for a solution to their problems. This very intelligent and compassionate agony aunt was convinced that most of them arrived at their sad sense of failure by unwittingly measuring themselves against fantasy images projected into their imaginations by story-tellers, script-writers, song-writers and advertisers. It hardly matters that no real woman in the history of the world ever actually possessed the characteristics of the glamorous ideal presented by the media: if that has become (probably without your knowing it) the desired self-image, then you will condemn yourself for failing to fulfil it. It hardly matters that no actual family in the history of the world has ever behaved like those in the commercials for breakfast cereals: at the back of your mind that fantasy can become the model by which the behaviour of your own family is judged – and condemned. 'What a bad mother I must be' may be too silly a conclusion ever to be spoken, but down at the level where guilt is nourished, the thought can be active.

Christian communicators are well aware of beliefs and codes which differ from their own and which they must counter, but they often seem less aware that the real enemies may be fantasies and images dwelling in the imagination rather than conscious opinions held in the head. Both the form and the content of Christian communication have to be adjusted to deal with these pictorial heresies, and in that connection it is worth spending a little time looking at the contribution which television may be making – not because its effects are necessarily undesirable, but because it does constitute a significant element in the mental climate around us all. And its image-making needs to be examined by those concerned with communicating conviction not because television is necessarily the medium through which to fight back (though I personally think it is an important one), but because the people in the pew and their neighbours in the streets around are all subject to these influences. To communicate with them we must understand them, and to understand them we must take account of the influence of television – and of its influence on the communicator, too.

And yet there seems to be no certainty as to what that influence is. I want to set two reports side by side and to delay identifying them until afterwards. The first is this.

Teachers, preachers, parents and legislators have asked us a thousand times over these past fifteen years whether violence in the media produces delinquency, whether the media raise or lower public taste, and just what the media can do to the political persuasions of their audiences. To these questions we have not only failed to provide definitive answers, but we have done something worse: we have provided evidence in partial support of every view of every hue.[1]

Now compare that verdict with this one.

Nobody can be sure about what television does to the viewer. One opinion holds that television programmes can subjugate whole populations and turn children into murderers. Another opinion holds that television is too trivial a cultural event to be considered. A surprising number of experts have subscribed to both these opinions in close succession or even simultaneously.[2]

Obviously there is a striking similarity between those two accounts. Yet the first – the one that was already looking back over fifteen years – was written by Joseph T. Klapper in 1957. The second was written by Clive James in 1981. The situation has changed little since then, so here is a period of more than forty years in which the influence of television has been expertly scrutinized with results which only tend to cancel each other out.

It is unlikely that a few paragraphs unbacked by research will achieve what professional sociologists have failed to achieve after much patient study, but I must say that their inconclusiveness could have something to do with their looking in the wrong direction. The tools they have been using do not seem to have been designed to reveal what is happening in the worlds of imagery and imagination. They have been tuned to measure changes in conscious opinions, in voting patterns, in purchasing patterns and in other forms of clearly observable action. Findings have been expressed in the form of statistics.

Surely that is not how human imagination is to be studied. 'Trace the influence of nineteenth-century impressionism on twentieth-century life-styles, and show your results in the form of statistical tables.' No examiner would dream of setting such a test. The impressionistic way of seeing may well have influenced us all, but since it did so by influencing our perceptions by way of our imaginations it is highly improbable that its effects can be expressed in numbers. And if it cannot be done for impressionism, why assume that it can be done for television? The information age may have to be denied its appetite for hard results in these areas where the subtle shaping of human imaginations is the subject of study.

This has been one of the problems of the Glasgow University Media Group. They are convinced that television in general and television news in particular are heavily biased against working people. They find significant evidence in the use of terms with differing emotive values, and in reports which contain implicit judgments on a situation – 'better news' about a rail strike, for instance, would probably mean that more trains were running. However, the Group has to earn its recognition as a professional unit in the world of sociology, so it quickly starts counting. And to me it seems that as the figures come in, the argument grows weaker.

It is, of course, quite possible to count the number of times a particular point of view is reported on the screen and to compare it with the number of times a differing point of view is represented. If the ratio is something like one to ten, that would seem like evidence of bias. But then there may be in fact not two possible positions on the issue but ten or more. In that case it could be right for any one point of view to have only a one in ten appearance. Those who hold that view may regard all alternatives as just one position: that of 'the people who disagree with us'. But if they disagree with each other as well, they will count differently. At once the simple, mathematical categories become inadequate. There is always someone able to undermine the evidence submitted in this form, and as a result the argument probably gets less attention than it deserves. The assumptions of the information age are again at work making us insensitive to the actual operations of human nature.

From a religious point of view we need, it seems to me, to take account of the influence of television in three different ways and at three different levels. I would suggest that television modifies human behaviour through persuasion, through imitation and through perception. And the greatest of these by far is perception.

22

Persuasion versus perception

To influence by persuasion is the explicit aim of party political broadcasting, of commercial advertising and of some forms of religious broadcasting. It could hardly be argued that all this is of no effect. Negatively, at least, it can be decisive. If product A is being advertised, then product B (its rival) cannot afford *not* to be advertised. If a totalitarian state compels all broadcasters to reflect the official point of view, their programmes may be received with much cynicism but viewers will remain unaware of any alternative interpretation of events. British party political broadcasts, though probably less influential than the political programmes which viewers regard as more impartial and therefore more truthful, have to be carefully balanced to see that no party with a legitimate claim to inclusion is in fact left out.

On the whole, however, the propagandist approach to television is not the one which has most influence – which is one, but only one, of the reasons why religious broadcasting does well to minimize it. The persuader relates to the uncommitted viewer in a way which is not altogether welcome. The viewer may resent being 'got at' when he or she is in no position to reply or to test what is being said. The transmission may well have an effect, but it is quite likely that its influence at the level of perception will be greater than its influence at the level of persuasion.

For instance, the commercial may fail to persuade you to buy a particular product, but it will have based its appeal on certain assumptions about what is good and desirable. That, too, is a message, though an unstated one. It is the vehicle of a value system, and it is quite possible to absorb that implicit message about the good life while rejecting the explicit message about the product. An interesting exercise is to sit through a batch of commercials deliberately excluding from attention the actual commodities being promoted, but mentally asking the promoter of each, 'On what grounds are you commending it? To what in me are you appealing? What are your assumptions about my life goals?' One researcher said long ago that these implicit sermons may well get under our guard.

As a matter of fact, the hidden message may be more important than the overt since this hidden message will escape the controls of consciousness, will not be 'looked through', will not be warded off by sales resistance, but is likely to sink into the spectator's mind.[3]

There have often been debates as to whether the persuaders actually create the value standards to which they appeal or whether they merely adopt the ones which are already there in the audience. From a practical and pastoral point of view it does not matter too much which of these is the case. The taken-for-granted values will extend their influence whether or not they are already present. Every time I am addressed on the unspoken and unnoticed assumption that my life goal is material prosperity or admiration or security, the more likely it is that this will be the truth about me. To defend myself against the process what I most need is to be aware of its happening. If I can see that I am being offered a view of life and not just an insurance policy, a view of human relationships and not just a hair shampoo, then I can be immunized. Otherwise what is likely to happen is that my actual perception of the world will be modified. I shall see life and measure it in terms of an unexamined assumption about the nature of the good.

One perception has been the subject of particular concern in recent years: that of the distinctive roles of men and of women. The churches are increasingly aware that their own treatment of the sexes within the life of the church has in the past owed more to social conditioning than it has to Christian theology. It is evidently important for us to know what stereotypes are being implanted. One journalist somewhat mischievously described the advertiser's idea of women in this way.

Women, according to the advertising industry, come in two types: young and not so young. The former are, it seems, maddeningly desirable, elusive and ambivalent. They are mainly employed as secretaries and other kinds of lackey to males, which lowly employment does not, however, prevent them from spending time on Caribbean beaches . . .

While lolling on such beaches, they are primarily engaged in smearing themselves in suntan lotion and drinking certain types of 'cosmetic' liquor. They are obsessed with personal hygiene – in particular the stemming of 'all-over perspiration' – and with the elimination of non-existent body fat . . .

Elusive creatures though they are, young advertising women are eventually trapped into marriage. Once they have been hunted, and secured by a resourceful male breadwinner, they are painlessly converted into the second type of advertising woman – the not-so-young housewife. But, having been seduced out of its chrysalis, this particular butterfly does not spread its wings and fly.

On the contrary: she breeds, exudes contentment, stays by the cooker and the kitchen sink, worries about domestic odours, washing up froth and the stains on her sons' rugby jerseys; becomes unable to tell the difference between margarine and butter, provides cereal, hot soup and mass-produced ravioli to her brood, and generally keeps the nuclear family show on the road . . .[4]

There are details in that account which begin to seem a little dated, but it was written in 1981 and much of it stands. Two years earlier two departments of Manchester University co-operated in the detailed examination of a week's output of commercials on Granada television. Inevitably they subjected their findings to statistical analysis, but given the relatively simple categories with which they were working, that seems to have been a viable operation. They found that the roles assigned to men and women – including the out-of-vision voices of men and women – were significantly different.

The nature of these differences was systematic and in accordance with traditional sex roles. Males were typically portrayed as having expertise and authority, as being objective and knowledgeable about reasons for buying particular products, as occupying roles which are autonomous, and as being concerned with the practical consequences of product purchase.

Females, on the other hand, were typically shown as consumers of products, as being unknowledgeable about the reasons for buying particular products, as occupying roles defined primarily in relation to other persons, and as being concerned with the social consequences of product purchase.[5]

If in the field of sex-typing, then in other fields too behaviour is likely to be affected by the way we are accustomed to having the world presented to us. Our own perceptions, and therefore our own attitudes and actions, can easily mirror those of the small screen. I am not suggesting that religious communicators should reply in kind. We neither can nor should embark on an expensive campaign to pour a stream of unexamined images into the imagination. Communicating conviction of the kind we care about is not to be achieved surreptitiously. Faith is not a conditioned reflex, it is the act of a whole human being exercising the whole range of human faculties – thought, will and imagination. Our calling is to bring people to life, not to lull them to sleep in the hope of moulding them through their dreams – as in Aldous Huxley's horrendous vision of a 'Brave New World'. However, one early step in the process of awakening may well be that of making people aware of the value systems being suggested to them, and being suggested even when the overt intention was only to get them to come out and vote, buy or worship.

Imitation versus perception

The process of suggestion needs to be examined not only in relation to programmes which set out to persuade, but all others as well. In the case of drama, news and documentary there are many who fear the force of imitation rather than that of deliberate persuasion. Mary Whitehouse's fear of undesirable behaviour patterns on the small screen is well known, and there are many who agree with her. Kenneth Oxford, Chief Constable of Merseyside, has an understandable fear of what he calls 'a daily diet of violent crime and brutality'. He spoke to a London conference about the influence of fictional 'cops and robbers' stories and suggested that that influence was not limited to those who imitated the criminals: 'Some young officers in the service also contribute to this macho image – they are not immune from mimicking the media conception or of enjoying "the thrill of the chase".'[6]

As with persuasion, there is no reason to deny that imitation can be one aspect of television's influence – especially when strong images of action are projected into a life that is dull, or into a personality which is a moral vacuum, or into a situation of discontent looking for a way of expressing itself. A member of Charles Manson's terrorist gang is reported to have said

> We are what you have made us. We were brought up on your TV. We were brought up watching Gunsmoke, Have Gun will Travel, FBI, Combat. Combat was my favourite show. I never missed Combat.[7]

Commenting on this, Conor Cruise O'Brien points out that to some extent violence has itself become a form of communication. Those who are given no media attention when they speak know that they will get it if they riot. Only the suppression of facts could prevent that, so the remedy has to be sought in other directions. I would think that there are two. One consists of a more determined attempt to see that people *are* heard when they speak. The other is to disseminate a wider and deeper understanding of the nature of violence. The latter will, however, involve dramatizing it. That is the classic way of examining such issues, as can be abundantly illustrated from the plays of Shakespeare.

Even Shakespeare's plays, however, can be alarming to those who are more concerned with imitation than they are with perception. In a theatrical anthology I found a reproduction of a playbill advertising the production of *Hamlet* in Kilkenny Theatre Royal on 14 May 1793. It contains the significant note: 'The parts of *the King and Queen*, by direction of the Rev. Father O'Callaghan, will be omitted, as too immoral for any stage.'[8]

Of course the good Father was entirely right that the behaviour of Shakespeare's king and queen is highly immoral. He was understandably alarmed at the possibility of his parishioners' behaving like that. But in Shakespeare's *Hamlet* the behaviour of the king and queen is very clearly *assessed* as being immoral. At the level of perception, as distinct from that of imitation, the influence of the play is a salutory one. It is not what a play is *about* which is of most significance, but the attitude it takes to what it is about. It can be about goodness and yet belittle it, or it can be about evil and reveal it for what it is. At the level of perception the former will be a harmful play and the latter a helpful one. To assess its value it is usually necessary to turn attention from the behaviour of the characters to the assessment of their behaviour by the author. In the acclaimed television drama serial (or series of television dramas if you prefer to stress the separateness of each episode), *The Boys from the Blackstuff*, unemployed workers in Liverpool were portrayed in a succession of sick stories. What was done and what was said were rarely admirable, but the tales were told with such compassion that viewing them was an enrichment of human experience.

Not that this principle – that it is all in the story-telling – has prevented people from trying to make characters into imitable models of desirable behaviour. I understand that in Mexico the popular serials usually referred to as 'soap operas' have been deliberately designed to encourage what is regarded as socially desirable behaviour. It is doubtless the government which decides what behaviour is socially desirable, but according to Peter Fiddick's report the whole exercise was carried out after careful research based on Bandura's social learning theory. The experts concluded that the method would work only if the stories were so arranged that socially desirable behaviour was immediately rewarded, and socially undesirable behaviour immediately punished. The fact that life does not behave like that must have been something of a problem to the writers – and even more of a problem to viewers if they were persuaded that this is the way the world is. However, a 23% increase in the sale of contraceptives was reported in the year that soap opera was dedicated to birth control.

Those who believe in the power of imitation can claim to have scored there, but it has to be said that other campaigns were running at the same time. Peter Fiddick's conclusion is that 'the soap operas imparted information but did not actually change the attitudes of the people who were their prime target'.[9] Where attitudes are concerned I think we must be in the realm of perception rather than imitation. Attitudes will be shaped by the values of the author rather than the behaviour of the characters. Perhaps the real and tacitly communicated value system of the Mexican soap operas was to be sought in a question to which I do not know the answer: what did they treat as a reward, and what as a punishment? That is where their assumptions about the good will have got across. And the chances are that nobody noticed – neither the broadcasters nor the viewers.

I emphasize the unobserved character of most communication about values and beliefs, because I think that here again the first step for the Christian communicator to take will often be that of getting people to become conscious of the process and to measure what they are offered by standards which *have* been examined and consciously approved. Sometimes the resulting judgment will be very favourable. I have myself had an entertaining time asking students to watch the comedy series, *Yes Minister*, and to list not *who* is being laughed at, but *what* is being laughed at. Until encouraged to think about it, it is easy to assume that politicians and civil servants are the only target, but a little reflection soon shows that many of our own follies are being shown up in all their absurdity. Vanity, ambition, a tendency to avoid answering the question until it becomes clear which answer is approved by those in authority: whoever laughs at these is laughing at what goes on in every home, in every school, in every college – and in every church. Appreciating that fact greatly enriches the joke, though it may also lead to an act of humble contrition before God. To see the joke in all its richness, however, the viewer must learn to *look* instead of assuming that the characters in the comedy are all that is being ridiculed.

Awareness is, however, only a first step. From analysis we must go on to action. In a way appropriate to our subject matter, our medium and our hearers we ourselves must communicate. The next three chapters will be concerned with the words, the stories and the pictures with which to do it, but what is already clear is that we are to project our message into a world of mental images. Our task is not primarily that of commending Christian doctrine against the rival appeal of other intellectual notions, or that of pouring Christian truth into minds which are open and empty. The field is already occupied. An imagination crowded with colourful figures and a mind attuned to a particular way of thinking is what awaits us. To be heard we shall need to be able to speak that language and yet be able to use it in the service of a truth revealed twenty centuries ago.

In doing so we shall help to heal the split in the soul of the twentieth century. We shall show that the highly symbolic fantasies which occupy twentieth-century imaginations, and the prosaic data which occupy twentieth-century thoughts, need not inhabit separated worlds. Incarnational faith finds that the real world actually *is* a symbolic expression of the transcendent. The data *are* poetry. Knowledge and imagination together are the servant of truth.

3

Words

Was it E. M. Forster who referred to 'poor little talkative Christianity'? He had a point. Historically Christians seem to have felt compelled to define the indefinable, to capture mystery in a verbal formula, to open their mouths and pour out explanations of everything. The author of Ecclesiastes was wiser. He knew that there is a time to be silent as well as a time to speak (Eccles. 3.7). What is more, the words which follow such a silence will themselves be marked by a certain reverence and restraint. They will not give the impression that they can *contain* God, only that they may point towards him. Gerhard Ebeling asks us to approach with this kind of reverence not only language about God, but all language.

> Since language is so intimately associated with life, something of the necessary reverence for life should be carried over to the way we use language. Our choice of speaking and silence should show that we are aware of the connection. When something is precious it must be guarded with particular care.[1]

Guarding the language in this way must surely include appreciating and respecting the way our native tongue has been used in the past to point to God. Not *every* hymn has to be a new one, and not every old one has to have its language up-dated. We can express our spiritual solidarity with a great tradition by taking the trouble to understand and use the songs, the prayers, the creeds of former times. But we cannot stop there. To keep the tradition alive we must clothe its essential faith in the language of our own time. And there we have difficulties.

The language of our time is ill-equipped to speak of God because it is not rich in symbolism. An earlier generation could sing 'Jesus, thy blood and righteousness, my glory are, my beauteous dress.' To many of us today this seems grotesque because we only half understand it to be symbolic. To speak of being dressed in someone's blood – or washed in it, or plunged in it – invites a number of quite unacceptably realistic images and ideas. We can substitute (with scriptural authority) the word 'life' for the word 'blood', but in many instances the rest of the statement then loses its force. 'Even intelligent people no longer understand the value and purpose of symbolical truth,' said C. G. Jung, 'and the spokesmen of religion have failed to deliver an apologetic suited to the spirit of the age.'[2]

One of those who might be regarded as an exception to Jung's rule was Bishop Ian Ramsey. He taught that the religious statements we need in order to convey our meaning must contain a 'model' and a 'qualifier'. The model would be described in that matter-of-fact language which is the natural idiom of our generation. The words would indicate some fact from within the range of those we can grasp. Then the qualifier would be added to the description in order to make the described event or object point beyond itself, become a symbol of some greatness in which it participates.

If I have got this right, to say that God is goodness is to provide a model without a qualifier. Goodness is an idea within our grasp, but to describe God simply as goodness is to make him only one more example of a familiar category – albeit the greatest example of it. On the other hand we could say that God is eternal, but that would be something like a qualifier without a model. We cannot grasp eternity. It is a concept beyond our conceiving and so the words convey almost nothing. But now add the two together: 'God is eternal goodness.' That's talking. It may be a less than inspired utterance, but at least it has the raw materials of a significant religious statement. It contains a concept we can grasp and an indication that this is part of something larger than we know. That, said Ramsey, is what we should look for in religious discourse.

If we want to understand language which claims to talk of mystery, if we want to understand some piece of distinctive religious discourse, we must first pick out the words which are most straightforward and most obviously descriptive. We then look at the other words to see which of them act as qualifiers behaving logically like an imperative to direct us to a disclosure. Every complete religious assertion will thus use words descriptively and also specify a technique by which we may move from 'what is seen' to 'what is seen and more', from the expressible to the point where the expressible becomes part of the inexpressible.[3]

If those who read are to find and interpret these double signals, then those who write must put them there. There would appear to be at least two approaches to this task.

Twinning

The first approach is to lay model and qualifier side by side. A shepherd's joy in the recovery of a lost sheep can be placed alongside heaven's joy in the recovery of a lost soul. The two experiences have a common parentage of which we are made aware. There is an invisible bond between them like that between twins. Making that bond perceptible is the art of religious language, and it is a difficult one – far easier to make the two independent statements and leave the parallels to meet one day in eternity.

Take first a fairly oblique example. During 1982 and 1983 a number of church assemblies and synods discussed the Christian attitude to nuclear weapons. Some of them, both British and American, were given many column-inches of reporting. The secular press must have been tempted to confine its reports to the bare bones of the political course advocated. 'No first use', would have been a natural summary of the resolution passed in London by the General Synod of the Church of England. ' "Ban the bomb", says church', would have been a fair headline over reports of the voting in the Assembly of the United Reformed Church. 'Kirk wants a freeze' was an actual and legitimate summary of the resolution passed in the General Assembly of the Church of

Scotland. All of this is accurate reporting, but clearly there is a element missing.

The editors of church magazines, on the other hand, might have been tempted to go the other way and to concentrate on the transcendent dimension of the debate in order to avoid hurting the political susceptibilities of their readership. A quite imaginary but plausible report might have started 'After much prayer and a thoughtful discussion the meeting reaffirmed its commitment to the Prince of Peace as the only answer to the world's need.' That too would have been an accurate piece of reporting, though again with a dimension missing.

The report which is hard to write – come to that, the debate which is hard to conduct – is the one which ties together both the practical decision and the sublime vision in the light of which it has to be made. The speakers were trying to relate a world of political realities to a world of eternal verities, trying to choose an option which is in practice available to the nations but to do so because it is the one most in harmony with – or at any rate, least alien to – a world greater than the one we know. It is far easier to report either of these two themes, or even both of them, than it is to report the connection between them.

Perhaps a start was made in one report in a national newspaper which quoted a speaker as saying, 'We are on the very edge of life itself and the total destruction of God's lovingly created universe is no longer unthinkable'.[4] That may not seem to get us very far, but to describe the universe as 'lovingly created' is to invest its physical existence with gracious purpose. The two dimensions are twinned. The discussion is at least given a reverent and theological context so that there is a possibility of moving 'from "what is seen" to "what is seen and more" ' – and back again.

If the giving of a cup of cold water is an act of transcendent significance, as Matthew 10.42 affirms that it is, then every act and object has its setting in eternity. It follows that to write truly of either the temporal or the eternal it is necessary to hold the two of them together. John Stewart Collis has contrived to write about the material creation in a factual way which is fully in accord with modern scientific knowledge and yet always reveals the universe to be a wonder and a mystery before which we must stand in awe and reverence as in the presence of God. One of his books is called *The Vision of Glory* but has also a sub-title: *The Extraordinary Nature of the Ordinary*.[5] It is the ordinary which is the substance of the vision of glory. To speak of glory without relating it to ordinariness, or to speak of ordinariness without relating it to glory, is to communicate the true character of neither.

But this discursive way is not the only method for combining model and qualifier. They can be brought together in single words, phrases or images which belong simultaneously to both the ordinary and the glorious. Language of this kind which spans the two worlds and makes the one speak of another is an example or extension of what is ordinarily known as metaphor or analogy or symbol. Without these, it seems, nothing that will communicate religious truth can ever be said.

Metaphor, analogy, symbol

Which of these terms is the correct one for a religious statement of this kind appears to be a point on which scholars differ. Professor G. B. Caird prefers 'metaphor'. He writes on *The Language and Imagery of the Bible*, but refers to the wider religious use of language of this kind.

> In its simplest form metaphor is the transfer of a name from its original referent to another; but this is commonly accompanied by a corresponding transference of feeling or attitude, and it is the second part of the process that makes metaphor such a potent influence in the emergence of moral ideas . . . We have no other language besides metaphor with which to speak about God.[6]

Professor John Macquarrie on the other hand regards the word 'metaphor' as applying only to a literary device for sharpening perception and revealing beauty. For the significant religious statement – the one which evokes commitment and joins the two worlds at a point where they really meet – he prefers the word 'analogy'. Speaking of God as Father is an instance of this because there is 'an intrinsic likeness between the analogue and that for which it stands'.[7]

According to Rosemary Haughton this would make it a suitable case for the word 'symbol'.

> A metaphor evokes a sense of one thing by reference to something other, which is comparable at certain points. It is the 'otherness' which makes metaphor possible and effective ... But a symbol is more than a metaphor, for it lives out of the thing it symbolizes; it is unlike and yet one with it . . .[8]

However, what is really interesting is not the respects in which these three writers differ in their usage, but their absolute unanimity about the nature of religious language. All insist that it must be language with a double meaning. The words have to have two applications, belong to two worlds with an intrinsic connection between them. Religious language has to be metaphorical, analogical, symbolic. And metaphor (if we adopt that term for it) is the language to which computers are deaf. Yet without it prophets, priests and theologians are dumb. As we have seen, it is not easy for the twentieth century to hear and understand words with these two natures. One of the first steps religious communicators must take is that of helping people to develop an ear for them, and we can begin by showing them that this kind of language is not only the language of the Bible, and not only the language of all religion, but also the language which is most distinctively human. Professor Sallie McFague says

> Metaphor is *the* way of human knowing. It is not simply a way of embellishing something we can know in some other way. There is no other way.[9]

This is because the metaphor takes hold of what is known and uses it to give meaning to what is not yet understood. Only in this way can imagination nourish understanding. It is along this path that human knowledge has advanced.

Where Christianity is concerned, this way with words is not only inescapable but is required by fidelity to its founder. Christ not only spoke in metaphors and parables – parables which have been described as extended metaphors – but was himself in a very real sense a living metaphor of God. Bishop John Tinsley has argued that we are bound to 'tell it slant' (an expression borrowed from the poetry of Emily Dickinson) because God himself, when he wished to communicate with us, did not do so *de haut en bas*, dropping his unanswerable and incomprehensible word upon us from above. Instead he was incarnate among us so that we, looking at that which was beside us, could see something of that which is above – a slanting, indirect sort of vision.

'Telling it slant' is more than an appropriate form of the gospel; it is its essential content, a manner incumbent upon the Christian communicator by the very nature of the Gospel. The Gospel is not only *what* is said, but *how* it is said . . . Frontal speech . . . besides being inimical to courtesy and tact in human relations, is profoundly foreign to a Christian mission that seeks its base in the manner of Christ.[10]

To acknowledge this to be the nature of Christian language might help the process of theological debate. It will not terminate such debates, because metaphor can be used to affirm what is false as well as what is true. Argument must go on as a way of testing the validity of what is being said, but if words are seen to be images rather than definitions they cannot so easily be used as weapons. Differing formulas defining (say) the chemical composition of water can only be at war with each other, but differing metaphors for God could both be true. Too often the contestants in theological discussion have seemed only too ready to clout each other with a form of words, as if their own terminology (or that of their standard of orthodoxy) captured the nature of God in a literal and definitive way. No such words can exist, but religious people are not immune to the tendency to handle religious language with less sensitivity and humility than it demands.

So we have to learn for ourselves as well as teach others the essentially symbolic and indirect nature of our language. However, in order to speak in that way we must learn to think in that way, and in order to think in that way we must learn to live in that way. And the first step is to recognize that this is the reality of the world around us. We can only speak in valid religious metaphors if the world actually *is* related to God in such a way as to provide the necessary mirrors. George Caird says that

Man begins with the familiar situations of home and community and derives from them metaphors to illuminate the activity of God; but the application of these terms to God establishes ideal and absolute standards which can be used as instruments for the remaking of man in God's likeness. Man is created to become like God, and the ultimate justification of anthropomorphic imagery lies in the contribution it makes to the attainment of that goal . . .

Thus anthropomorphism is something more than the imposing of man's preconceived and limited images on the divine. There is something that answers back in perpetual dialogue and criticism.[11]

Without this 'something that answers back', metaphor would be mere fancy. It can be used with conviction only by those who possess what Aidan Nichols calls 'a sense of the world as carrying the power and radiance of significant presence, under a law of participation and exchange'.[12] More directly still James D. Smart, summarizing the use of analogical methods of interpretation in the work of Karl Barth, says that 'the source of the analogies between events on earth lies in the fact that all historical events have their origin in God's own life within the Godhead in eternity.'[13]

To communicate in such a world on behalf of such a God it is first of all necessary for the communicator to relate to the creation in such a way that it is actually experienced as the medium of living contact between ourselves and God. It is not enough to believe that this is the case and to make up metaphors to illustrate it. The communicator needs to perceive all objects and events in this light, to see the world as it is and then to speak as he or she sees. Radio producers tell radio talks broadcasters that it is not enough clearly to articulate the words of a carefully prepared script. The broadcaster must while speaking re-experience whatever it was that caused the script to be written in the first place. What is described must there and then be re-perceived in the telling, whatever was felt or understood must there and then be felt or grasped afresh.

The same sort of thing is true of other forms of communication. The communicator does not just deliver packets of information.

He or she draws the hearer into an experience. To do that the communicator must also be experiencing, and for the Christian that means being alive at all times to the sacramental significance of the world around us. Then the metaphors can be perceptions and not just literary devices. The underlying experience can become a shared experience, and the interpretation of that experience can become a shared understanding of religious truth. The classic perception – one from which metaphors flow as naturally as rivers run – is that of Thomas Traherne, and he said that 'your enjoyment of the world is never right, till every morning you awake in heaven: see your self in your father's palace, and look upon the skies and the earth and the air as celestial joys'.[14] Given such a perception of the world, it should be possible to draw modern knowledge and new experiences into the task of imaging the divine.

New ways with words

New metaphors are not to be invented but discovered. They are already there in the nature of reality. The metaphor, unlike the simile, is derived from an intrinsic connection between the two spheres to which it refers. But if the world is still related to God in the way Traherne thought it to be in the seventeenth century, then the necessary connections do exist. Genuinely new hymns should enrich the great tradition. Authentic symbols of the transcendent should be discovered daily, even in the world of the computer. Do ROM and REM themselves mirror two different aspects of divine providence? Does cybernetics demonstrate the inhuman methods of control which God refuses to employ on human beings? People deeply immersed in both the world of technology and the world of the Spirit may yet express traditional doctrines in new ways which carry conviction to the modern community. But they must not start with the traditional formulations and merely translate them or illustrate them with modern jargon. They must first actually experience the connection as they live fully in the two worlds. We are not called to speak with forked tongue, but we are called to speak from within the experience of double vision.

When the Christian communicator speaks from outside that experience, the bond between the two worlds is broken. And this applies, as Bishop Tinsley reminded us, not only to *what* is said but also to *how* it is said. It is possible even by the manner in which words are used to suggest detachment from one world or the other. At one time the ecclesiastical manner tended to suggest the imparting of a heavenly truth unsullied by any contact with earthly realities. The parsonical voice itself seemed to echo some form of angelic chanting inaudible to the rest of us. When I first started work as a radio producer nearly thirty-five years ago, it was regarded as a regular part of the job to try and get clerical broadcasters to sound a bit more like human beings.

By the time I was due to retire from television the situation was very different. The parsonical voice was generally to be found only in comedians imitating other comedians' imitations of the parsonical voice. The actual religious broadcaster sounded much more human – sometimes only too human. In both style and content the religious broadcaster could by then be so down to earth that the earth remained earthy, hardly at all an image of glory. So the bonding of time and eternity can be broken apart not only by the mannerisms of the high and holy-sounding broadcaster of old, but also by those of his successors whose style is more like that of a newsreader on a day when there is not much significance in the news.

Since language is the subject of this chapter, the radio talk provides a natural area in which to examine words in their spoken form. A characteristic list of recommendations from a radio producer to the giver of a broadcast talk might run something like this.

1. Define your objective. Be clear about what you want to do for the listener. Make it an aim high enough to be worth attempting, but not so high as to be beyond attainment. Work within the limitations of the medium, but stretch them.

2. Work from the particular to the general and not the other way round. Universal truths are communicated through particular instances, and it is only when the particular seed has been implanted that the universal can grow out of it.

3. Use spoken English, and use it as a vehicle of your own

40

personality: short sentences; verbs rather than abstract nouns; phrases which are alive with your own life rather than forms of words from which you are yourself detached.

4. Personalize without being egocentric. The listener is not to be drawn to yourself but invited to share your own appreciation of some aspect of the life around you both. A personal relationship between broadcaster and listener is possible, but as the broadcaster you should be aware that the relationship is essentially a triangular one between you, the listener and the subject. Do not seek an eyeball to eyeball meeting: invite the hearer to look at what you see.

5. Do not antagonize the listener by claiming a knowledge of him or her which you do not in fact possess ('At this point you will say . . .') or by filling the script with rhetorical questions which the listener would like to treat as non-rhetorical if only this were two-way communication. Never abuse your monopoly of utterance.

6. Provide sign-posts and boundary lines within your script, but beware of abrupt gear changes as when an amusing incident is used as a mere springboard to a metaphysical speculation having no intrinsic connection with the introductory ploy.

7. In the opening moments persuade the listener that it will be a good idea to go on listening either because you have raised a question to which he really needs to hear an answer, or because what you have to say promises real entertainment.

This mostly secular advice has already many of the characteristics demanded of a communication derived from the Christian incarnation model. Its demand for concreteness is in harmony with belief in a word made flesh. Its demand for a personal stance and style is in harmony with belief in the human as an image of the divine. Its demand that the independence and responsibility of the listener be respected is in harmony with belief in what a Quaker would call 'that of God in every man'. Its demand for the continuity of the secular and the religious accords with belief in the sacramental, and therefore metaphorical nature of all experience.

This congruence between Christian doctrine and radio experience is only to be expected if both Christian doctrine and radio experience are giving true accounts of how human life actually functions. Both the religious broadcaster and the non-religious broadcaster are pushed towards language which is a product of double vision. It will be simultaneously subjective and objective, simultaneously particular and universal, simultaneously concrete and metaphysical. It will in fact be a description of the world and of human life as they appear when each detail is seen to be a metaphor of a larger whole – to the religious speaker a temporal metaphor of the eternal, of heaven or of hell.

As an example of the latter here are a couple of paragraphs by Paul Yates from his contribution to *The Light of Experience* – a television series which has much in common with radio talks in that it has as its core a spoken monologue.

> I remember coming out of a bar deep in the heart of Belfast. Leaning on the corner to smoke a cigarette I looked up and down the street. Row after row of shop windows and doorways bricked up, boarded up, filled in. Everything was sunk in a pale grey light, not a soul in sight. A discarded newspaper blew across the road, clouds of dust followed from nearby demolition sites. A stray dog trotted nervously along the pavement. In the distance I could hear the sound of gunfire and ambulance sirens.
>
> The dog stopped beside me, its ears leaned back in the direction of the guns and sirens. It began a low almost imperceptible howl which gradually got louder. The howl came in unison with the ambulance sirens. The dog's body trembled, its head moved from side to side unable to understand what had triggered the howling mechanism in its brain. Its eyes were filled with fear and confusion. It looked up at me but saw no answers. The buses were off, the trains were off. Not a soul in sight. Just me and this dog howling at my feet. The whole scene took on a sense of inertia like it was a dream or a nightmare. Everything dirty, everything ruined. Each of us trapped under a sky made of stone. Confused. Unable to move. Unable to understand. Howling.[15]

Every sentence in these paragraphs offers the hearer a visible detail of a particular scene, and every detail stands for something more than itself. The whole scene and every detail in it are visible metaphors evoked in words and found in the raw material of the present day. A different scene – conceivably even the same scene described in a different way – could be affirmative where this is negative, an image of heaven instead of hell. But it would have to have been experienced that way – in the real world of the imagination if not in the real world of personal autobiography. The making of new metaphors is not easy.

Renewing old ways with words

A dead metaphor, in George Caird's use of the term, is an old one which no longer works as a means of conveying feelings and attitudes from one area to another. Its characteristic is that the original, down-to-earth meaning of the term is forgotten and the word is used as if it were not metaphorical but realistic. For instance, Christians sometimes talk about redemption as if it were a technical and accurate theological term carrying no overtones from the world of pawnbrokers or of slavery.

In fact, of course, a New Testament writer using the verb 'to redeem' was using a term in everyday use among the high proportion of his readers who were either slaves or slave-owners. It meant being set free from the humiliating legal status of slavery. It was a word drenched in hope and fear before ever it was applied to Christian experience. So when Paul wrote that 'God sent forth his Son, made of a woman, made under the law, to redeem them that were under the law, that we might receive the adoption of sons' (Gal. 4.4–5), the people to whom he wrote will have been vividly aware that 'to redeem' was a metaphor (as also, incidentally, were 'sonship' and 'adoption'). It enabled them to release in a new direction all the pent up feelings associated with the more normal usage of the term. To those of us for whom the religious usage *is* the normal one the word does not speak with such power.

It is possible, however, that to think ourselves back into the position of the first recipients of the letter is easier than to find an alternative image in modern experience. In fact it might be possible to lead a modern audience even farther back into history and to find them positively enjoying the mental effort required to give back life to old language. They will remember (if only through Handel's *Messiah*) Job's phrase: 'I know that my redeemer liveth.'

In this case the word is a translation of the Hebrew 'goel', and that word can be found elsewhere with other translations. In the story of Ruth, for instance, it is translated 'kinsman'. Naomi says that Boaz is 'goel' to her and to Ruth. The word refers to a law under which a man's nearest relative was obliged to come to his aid if he fell into debt and to accept responsibility for his widow if he died. The New International Version brings both translations together and speaks of Boaz as 'kinsman-redeemer'.

This may seem all very academic, but let the imagination play with this history and enjoy it. Paul uses a term which for him points towards Christ as his 'kinsman-redeemer'. The metaphor speaks not only of Christ's releasing me but also of his kinship to me – 'made of a woman, made under the law'. It is an image resonant with Christmas as well as with Passiontide and Easter. Compared with the riches to be found in such old, dead metaphors some of the modern alternatives seem a bit impoverished.

It has been suggested, for instance, that we now know too much about optics for 'light' to be the strong metaphor which it was in New Testament times – a point of view expressed long ago by Keats in his sad comment on what Newton had done to the rainbow by explaining it. As an alternative to 'light' we have been offered 'openness'. It is a good word and not without useful resonances, but it is hard to believe that it could do the work which the image of light has done in the past and offers to do afresh at the dawning of each day. Better, I should think, to delve deeper into the wonder of light as Newton described it, bring the metaphor to life by working harder on it. In the book by John Stewart Collis to which I have already referred there is an account of light and colour which makes them seem *more* magical and awesome than was the rainbow in the pre-Newtonian days of Keats' imagination. It may be paradoxical but it could well be the task of the Christian communicator to make people more aware of the facts and workings of the physical world in order to be more sensitive to its spiritual significance.

A generation starved of significant symbols is more likely to stuff itself with insignificant ones than to do without them altogether. In the realms of fantasy the extra-terrestrial takes the place of the transcendent. Lacking the concept of an eternal world which embraces and includes the present one, people turn to the idea of a world which is just a long way off from this one. They imagine all kinds of wonders coming from it – horrors sometimes, but saviours too: peacemakers, speakers of eternal truth.

I end this chapter by making a free gift of an idea worth millions to anybody who has the ear of a film magnate. What audiences hunger for are the mechanical devices of science fiction plus the symbolic significance of the great myths and religions. So here is a formula. Start with a visitor from outer space. Any hack script-writer can knock up that part of the story. The director and his technicians will make it compulsive viewing. The difficult bit comes when the visitant has to communicate with the terrestrials. He must not do it in the prosy language of everybody's breakfast table. He needs to speak in such a way as to open the audience's minds wider than their eyes have been opened to the galaxies. No hack script-writer will come up with the dialogue required, so why not use what is already at hand?

Take, for instance, a few pages from Kahlil Gibran's *The Prophet*. It is more or less in the form of dialogue already: 'A woman said, Speak to us of Joy and Sorrow ... Then said a teacher, Speak to us of Teaching ... And a poet said, Speak to us of Beauty ...' and so on. So it can be the best-looking girl in the entire cast who gets the line 'Speak to us of love.' She thus opens the sluice gates to a torrent of symbols deeply religious in character and yet (given the context) as welcome to a cinema audience as rain in a land of drought.

> When love beckons to you, follow him,
> Though his ways are hard and steep.
> And when his wings enfold you yield to him,
> Though the sword hidden among his pinions may wound you.
> And when he speaks to you believe him,
> Though his voice may shatter your dreams as the north wind lays waste the garden.
>
> . . . . .
>
> For even as love crowns you so shall he crucify you. Even as he is for your growth so is he for your pruning.

Even as he ascends to your height and caresses your tenderest branches that quiver in the sun,

So shall he descend to your roots and shake them in their clinging to the earth.

Like sheaves of corn he gathers you unto himself.

He threshes you to make you naked.

He sifts you to free you from husks.

He grinds you to whiteness.

He kneads you until you are pliant;

And then he assigns you to his sacred fire, that you may become sacred bread for God's sacred feast.[16]

4

Stories

A chapter on story-telling should begin with an example. Here is a story which has a title and a sub-title. For reasons which will become clear I hold back the sub-title until after the tale is told.

The Skylark and the Frogs

There was once a society of frogs that lived at the bottom of a deep, dark well, from which nothing whatsoever could be seen of the world outside. They were ruled over by a great Boss Frog, a fearful bully who claimed, on rather dubious grounds, to own the well and all that creeped or crawled therein. The Boss Frog never did a lick of work to feed or keep himself, but lived off the labors of the several bottom-dog frogs with whom he shared the well. They, wretched creatures! spent all the hours of their lightless days and a good many more of their lightless nights drudging about in the damp and slime to find the tiny grubs and mites on which the Boss Frog fattened.

Now, occasionally an eccentric skylark would flutter down into the well (for God only knows what reason) and would sing to the frogs of all the marvelous things it had seen in its journeyings in the great world outside: of the sun and the moon and the stars, of the sky-climbing mountains and fruitful valleys and the vast stormy seas, and of what it was like to adventure the boundless space above them.

Whenever the skylark came visiting, the Boss Frog would instruct the bottom-dog frogs to attend closely to all the bird had to tell. 'For he is telling you,' the Boss Frog would explain, 'of the happy land whither all good frogs go for their reward when they finish this life of trials.' Secretly, however, the Boss Frog (who was half deaf anyway and never very sure of what the lark was saying) thought this strange bird was quite mad.

Perhaps the bottom-dog frogs had once been deceived by what the Boss Frog told them. But with time they had grown cynical about such fairy tales as the skylark had to tell, and had reached the conclusion also that the lark was more than a little mad. Moreover, they had been convinced by certain free-thinking frogs among them (though who can say where these freethinkers come from?) that this bird was being used by the Boss Frog to comfort and distract them with tales of pie in the sky which you get when you die. 'And that's a lie' the bottom-dog frogs bitterly croaked.

But there was among the bottom-dog frogs a philosopher frog who had invented a new and quite interesting idea about the skylark. 'What the lark says is not *exactly* a lie,' the philosopher frog suggested. 'Nor is it madness. What the lark is really telling us about in its own queer way is the beautiful place we might make of this unhappy well of ours if only we set our minds to it. When the lark sings of sun and moon, it means the wonderful new forms of illumination we might introduce to dispel the darkness we live in. When it sings of the wide and windy skies, it means the healthful ventilation we should be enjoying instead of the dank and fetid airs we have grown accustomed to. When it sings of growing giddy with its dizzy swooping through the heavens it means the delights of the liberated senses we should all know if we were not forced to waste our lives at such oppressive drudgery. Most important, when it sings of soaring wild and unfettered among the stars, it means the freedom we shall all have when the onus of the Boss Frog is removed from our backs forever. So you see: the bird is not to be scorned. Rather, it should be appreciated and praised for bestowing on us an inspiration that emancipates us from despair.

Thanks to the philosopher frog, the bottom-dog frogs came to have a new and affectionate view of the skylark. In fact, when the revolution finally came (for revolutions always do come), the bottom-dog frogs even inscribed the image of the skylark on their banners and marched to the barricades doing the best they could in their croaking way to imitate the bird's lyrical tunes. Following the Boss Frog's overthrow, the once dark, dank well was magnificently illuminated and ventilated and made a much more comfortable place to live. In addition, the frogs experienced a new and gratifying leisure with many attendant delights of the senses – even as the philosopher frog had foretold.

But *still* the eccentric skylark would come visiting with tales of the sun and the moon and the stars, of mountains and valleys and seas, and of grand winged adventures it had known.

'Perhaps,' conjectured the philosopher frog, 'this bird *is* mad, after all. Surely we have no further need of these cryptic songs. And in any case, it is very tiresome to have to listen to fantasies when the fantasies have lost their social relevance.'

So one day the frogs contrived to capture the lark. And upon so doing, they stuffed it and put it in their newly built civic (admission-free) museum . . . in a place of honor.[1]

Now that you have enjoyed the story I can reveal the sub-title so that you will know on what abstruse matters you have been pondering: 'The Skylark and the Frogs: A Postscript to Herbert Marcuse's Philosophical Inquiry into Freud, Freely Adapted from the Fable by Chuang-tzu'. The story is part of Theodore Roszak's *The Making of a Counter Culture*.

What is significant is that while reading the story you almost certainly *did* think about the heavy issues of the sub-title – and it didn't hurt a bit. You must at least have looked beyond the frogs to human history, human nature, the life of the church. As communicators, stories work where concepts fail. To set out to communicate conviction and yet to deny yourself the narrative method would make as much sense as having your legs amputated before entering for the marathon.

Yet the story is a dangerous instrument. It does not always communicate the conviction intended by the story-teller, and it can delude both the teller and the hearer into believing that much has been communicated when very little in fact has. The well-known appetite of adult congregations for children's addresses in story form may conceal a preference for the undemanding which, if satisfied, could build up a positive resistance to the exacting challenge of the gospel.

Above all there is the difficulty that different stories relate to truth and convey their convictions in quite different ways. If the story-teller is working in one idiom and the hearers are listening in another, then what is communicated may be false and harmful. A cautionary tale such as that of Jonah needs to be told and heard for what it is. When it is told in such a way that it could be either a cautionary tale or a historical miracle story, the teller can be accused of careless communication and the hearer can be quite deceived about the truth in the tale.

So it is a matter of importance to try and clarify the different ways in which narrative can embody truth. The names used for the various categories to be considered here are not important. Specialists may say that I use some of the terms wrongly, but I am only concerned with the variety of ways in which a story can communicate conviction. It seems to me that story-tellers need to know and to make known which idiom is being used in a particular case. That is not a matter of giving it an appropriate label from a catalogue of literary forms but of actually telling the tale in such a way that its particular mode of conveying truth is clear at the receiving end. The labels I shall use are documentary (or history), myth, paradigm, legend, parable, allegory, illustration and example. Change the labels if you wish, but let the different kinds of story-telling be respected.

Documentary

There are some historical narratives for which factual accuracy is of primary importance. The events recorded in one of Aesop's fables need never have taken place – *could* never have taken place. It doesn't matter. But if Jesus did not actually die by crucifixion, that matters. An incarnational faith must rest on real events. The hard documentary element in the Christian story must be told for what it is – and received for what it is. Otherwise the revelation of God has yet to reach us in flesh and blood fact.

And the narration of revealing events is still the primary form of Christian communication. Christianity is not a set of concepts or doctrines which can conveniently be illustrated from history. The history is prior to the concept, prior to the doctrine. Christian ideas are the fruit of subsequent reflection on events. It is the events themselves which convey the revelation. In present day communication, too, the narrative should still have priority over the notion. 'Narrative theology' is now a respectable theological category, but should not be confined to the study of the Old Testament. All theology is primarily narrative. The cycle of the church year, with the story-telling embodied in it, probably does more to Christianize our culture than any amount of moralizing or arguing.

At the same time as relating the story of events the Christian communicator must, however, make clear the significance of those events. Even documentary history is never bare documentary. The New Testament (like the church year) tells of events in such a way as to make them also symbols. A well-known broadcaster, anchor-man of many a quizz and panel game on radio and television, once said something like this about the Gospels: 'What I want to know is whether all this is documentary or poetry.' It is, of course, both – not partly one and partly the other, but simultaneously both. The events themselves have the symbolic quality of great poetry. They *have* to be told as such.

After all, even so solidly historical an affirmation as 'suffered under Pontius Pilate' merits its place in the creed only if that particular moment of suffering concentrates in itself all the longing and the poetry of the classic myth of the dying god. History it is, but it has to be narrated in a way which adds the emotive power of myth and symbol to the documentary fact of crucifixion – not in order to garnish a bare fact with pious fancy, but in order to tell the truth about what really happened. According to Rosemary Haughton this approach seems distinctly odd to the typical modern mind.

My approach to the Gospels ... may strike some as naive, since it is based on the assumption that all four evengelists were writing about things actually seen and heard (not necessarily by themselves, of course, but by witnesses) and using whatever poetic categories of religious and historic imagery they needed to clarify the nature of what was seen and heard.

The assumption of many exegetes seems to be that one cannot do *both* these things. Either one reports something actually seen with the bodily eyes or heard with the ears, or one evokes an inner experience by means of relevant symbols and associations.[2]

It is not only the exegetes, however, who make this separation. One of the difficulties with biblical dramatization is that general audiences tend to do the same. Dramatize the story of Moses or of Jesus on the television screen and you find that events and dialogue can be reproduced with great fidelity to the text, but the story will fail to speak to any who do not bring to it the prior ability to read the symbolism in the happenings. There is a kind of inevitable literalism in the presentation which is not easily overcome, and it is due to the fact that the biblical narrator has been removed. His narrative is there, but not his reasons for telling it, not his understanding of its meaning. The underlying assumptions which once bound the teller and the hearer and provided the context of the story are no longer shared. The modern audience is unaware of what questions are being answered and is therefore unaware of what convictions are being offered. Instead of asking 'What does this mean?', it asks only 'Did this really happen?' If the answer is (referring, say, to a Cecil B. De Mille-type crossing of the Red Sea) 'Well, something happened but it may not have been just like that', then the story will be dismissed as simply untrue. If the answer is (referring, say, to Jesus's praying for the forgiveness of those who crucified him) 'Yes, it did', then the story is true but not necessarily significant in life today. Costume drama remains costume drama. The news will follow in a few minutes.

So the Christian story-teller has to work, and be known to work, in an idiom where facts are both sacred and symbolic. It is another version of Bishop Ramsey's 'model and qualifier' principle, but in story-telling both may take narrative form and may therefore be difficult to distinguish from one another. The same story is likely to contain accurate reporting and also details which are there not so much as part of the record of what happened but as signifying the meaning of what happened. It may rarely be necessary to draw a clear line between the two elements, but the story must be told in such a way that both kinds of listening take place or the listener will miss either the documentary data or the transcendent qualifiers. It is, given the assumptions and attitudes of our day, a difficult and sophisticated form of story-telling.

Perhaps the best hope of getting it generally understood is to invite attention to the narrator as well as the narration. Luke's story of the birth of Christ is solely Luke's. To tell it as if it might just as well have been narrated that way by Mark or by Paul or by the reporter from *The Guardian* newspaper is to rob it of its proper values and to import different ones into it. The story has to be heard firstly as coming from Luke, coloured by all the poetry and symbolism of his mind. It has to be heard secondly as coming through a present-day communicator who has tried to look through Luke's eyes and then respond in twentieth-century terms to what so moved Luke when he first heard the story himself.

Myth

That some of the qualities of myth have to be retained in the telling of history has already been said, but myth can also be a vehicle of truth when it is nothing but myth – when the factual and documentary element is entirely absent. Consider this story, for instance.

> Once upon a time, the Moon sent an insect to men, saying, 'Go to men and tell them, "As I die and dying live, so you shall also die and dying live!"'
>
> The insect started off with the message, but as it was going on its way it was overtaken by the hare who asked, 'Where are you going?'
>
> The insect answered, 'The Moon has sent me as a messenger to men, to tell them that as she dies and dying lives, so shall they also die and dying live.'
>
> The hare said, 'As you are slow and an awkward runner, let

me go.' With these words he ran off, and when he came to the place where men lived, he said, 'I am sent by the Moon to tell you, "As I die and wholly perish, in the same way you also shall die and come to an end." '

The hare then returned to the Moon and told her what he had said to men. The Moon scolded him, saying, 'Do you dare to tell the people a thing which I have not said?'

With these words the Moon picked up a piece of wood and struck the hare on the nose. Since that day the hare's nose has been split, but men still believe what he told them.[3]

That Hottentot story from South Africa: is it – answer yes or no as the quizz master insists you must – true or false? The quizz master cannot be obeyed. The question does not permit of that kind of answer. In one sense the tale is clearly a nonsense. In another sense it is very true. Its picture of the human condition is deadly accurate. In this case it is unlikely that people today would make the mistake of thinking the story to be true in the documentary sense. It is more likely that they would think it untrue in any sense. But to lose the capacity to detect the value of such non-documentary narratives is to lose an ability which is much needed for the full appreciation of religious truth – even, according to Patrick Henry, of New Testament truth.

The gift that religion can offer people today is not demythologization, but a renewal of the sense of mystery that is conveyed only in myth. If you demythologize the New Testament, people will look elsewhere for what you have eliminated, and the wide popularity of Tolkien's Middle Earth, of Lewis's Narnia, of *Watership Down*, of *Star Wars*, of science fiction itself, suggests that modern persons are quite sophisticated about myth, and hungry for it.[4]

Whether myths are interpreted in a Jungian way as projections of something deep in the human psyche, or in a structuralist way as exhibiting the codes and standards of a particular society, myths seem always to be concerned to meet a need. Roger Silverstone has written that 'The myths are basically answers to questions, and the questions and to a degree the answers also, are the universal ones of human existence.'[5] He is interpreting the work of Levi-Strauss, but it is significant that he is doing it in a book about television. He argues that television is making our society more like one of the communities within which the myths evolved than it is like the society of recent generations in which information and ideas were passed from one to another via the printed word. After all, the dominant mode of communication is now once again oral rather than written, it speaks simultaneously to the group rather than at different times to different individuals, and it is essentially narrative in form. Every report is 'a story'. So it is not impossible that modern technology could make us at heart a more primitive society.

Perhaps the real issue is whether we are going to satisfy our appetite with trivial myth-substitutes such as soap operas, or whether we can be nourished by the great myths and thus prepared to receive the even greater truths of revelation. The Nordic myths played their part in preparing C. S. Lewis for conversion to Christianity, and it is hard to believe that such a story as that of Baldur the Beautiful (slain by envy and kept by Hel until all shall weep for him) would not enrich anyone's response to the crucifixion of Christ.

What is important is to distinguish this particular one among the different ways in which narrative can relate to truth, and to recognize the degree to which the Christian communicator is necessarily involved with the language and the values of myth.

> The mythical origin of most of the primary symbols of religious expression is historically beyond question. Even the most spiritual symbols of the most moralized religions have their source in the womb of the unconscious out of which the myth and its symbols have been born. The most exalted idiom of theology no less than the language of purest devotion makes use of this treasury of the ages.[6]

Paradigm

Throughout the Old Testament the story of the Exodus from Egypt is told not only as ancient history but as a story providing norms of behaviour relevant to the time of the story-teller. 'Thou shalt neither vex a stranger, nor oppress him: for ye were strangers in the land of Egypt' (Ex. 22.21). And so on. The experience of slavery and the story of liberation have become the means of communicating standards. That, as I understand it, is characteristic of the paradigm. As a story it may relate to historical events, but more important than its historical accuracy is its normative value. It tells you what you are and therefore how you should live.

> In the Hebrew and Christian Scriptures, the narrative mode has extraordinary importance, and not only quantitatively. If one looks at the classics and characters of other religions or religious philosophies, the story aspect may be relatively marginal. Their sacred books often take the form of oracular aphorism or philosophical instruction or mystical treatise or didactic code. In the case of biblical man, language moved towards recital, and all heaven and earth came into it.[7]

That is the judgment of a notable authority, Amos N. Wilder. He insists that in the case of the New Testament particularly the nature of the gospel required the narrative form.

> That story telling had such a central place in the very beginning of the Gospel means more than may at first appear. It is not enough to say that Jesus used the form of the parable only as a good pedagogical strategy. It was not merely to hold the attention of his hearers that he told stories or took good illustrations out of his file. There was something in the nature of the case that evoked this rhetoric, something in the nature of the Gospel.[8]

The necessity of narrative arises from the fact that it is events which are significant, and it is important to relate those events in such a way that their significance is revealed in the telling. To tell the tale and then add a moral as appendix is hardly better than starting with a concept and using the story to illustrate it. Either way meaning is detached from narrative. The story becomes little more than an attention-holder. The real lesson is in propositional form and is therefore less likely to be communicated effectively.

Yet telling a story so that its intrinsic paradigmatic value is revealed in the narrative can be difficult. Imagination is called for at both the transmitting end and the receiving end. Often it is a matter of describing some character in the story in such a way that the listener can see something of himself or herself in that character, or of describing an event in such a way that the hearer can see something of our own time in the situation. It is achieved by listening for the intention of the original story-teller and then serving that intention so faithfully that it stirs up resonances in the world of today.

It should be possible, for instance, to describe the Old Testament character of Naaman the Syrian in such a way that in spite of his alien culture and his leprosy we feel for ourselves the naturalness of his disappointment when the prophet Elisha merely sends a messenger to tell him to wash in the river Jordan. He wanted divine power to manifest itself through its agent in a much more spectacular way. 'I thought, He will surely come out to me, and stand, and call on the name of the Lord his God, and strike his hand over the place . . .' We all have our own ideas of how a religious act should be performed. Naaman's comment, if the way for it is properly prepared, does not even have to be translated out of the Authorized Version. Nor should it really be necessary to substitute the Thames and the Mersey for the original rivers of his derisive comparison: 'Are not Abana and Pharpar, rivers of Damascus, better than all the waters of Israel?' (II Kings 5.11–12). Modernize the story too much and it loses its plausibility. After all, we do not actually suffer from leprosy and would not be well advised to bathe in some reaches of either Thames or Mersey. It is easier to get back to Naaman's time (or rather, that of his narrator) and to find our own prejudices under Naaman's skin than it is to up-date his story and retain its force as paradigm.

Legend

I once heard a well-meaning guide in Verona pointing out that most unfortunately Shakespeare had got the story of Romeo and Juliet all wrong. That is *not* what happened at the mating of Montague and Capulet. We English were supposed to feel mortified on behalf of our national poet. But who cares? There is more beauty and more truth in Shakespeare's fiction than in a whole city full of fact. Historical inaccuracy can be a valuable servant of more fundamental truth – so long as the recipients know what they are getting.

According to Renan this can even apply to historical characters of considerable religious significance, such as the saints.

> An anecdotal and legendary history can be truer than truth itself, for the glory of the legend belongs to the man who has known how to inspire his humble admirers with the values that, without him, they would never have discovered.[9]

The stories of St Francis to be found in almost contemporary biographies are sometimes fairly unconvincing as reportage, but what a man Francis must have been to inspire such tales! As for the *Canticle of the Sun*, either he wrote it (in which case he was a great man) or he inspired one of his followers to write it (in which case he was arguably an even greater man). The true Francis comes through the legends genuinely alive if inaccurately reported.

A legend can even be a vehicle of truth when its central character's very existence is unproven. St Christopher is a very hazy figure to the historian, but in the *Golden Legend* he not only carries Christ on his back but tests the alternative claims of wealth, of force, of evil. The story is not only significant but pertinent. The truth about the twentieth century is there. But the twentieth century is unlikely to receive that truth in this form unless an appropriate style of story-telling is used. It is not just a matter of relating the incidents clearly. There is need for a special manner to match and to make clear the nature of the narrative. Just as 'Once upon a time . . .' sets the mood of a story to be told in the key of magic, or 'In the dream time . . .' that of Aboriginal myth, so the idiom of legend requires a certain decorative and almost liturgical style. Deliberately antique language does not help, but there are devices which do: the repetition of a formal phrase in the dialogue, the repetition in a variety of settings of a cycle of events in the action. These suggest that significance is to be sought less in the events than in the telling. They can alert those at the receiving end of the communication as to the nature of the narrative and so the direction in which truth is to be looked for.

Anthony Burgess is a modern novelist who is well aware of the distinction between truth and what he calls 'factuality'. In *Earthly Powers* the central character, a novelist, is asked to give evidence of an alleged miracle at which he had been present. His testimony may determine whether or not his former friend is officially declared to be a saint. So he realizes that he must be 'less concerned now with that deeper truth, the traditional attribute of God, which literature can best serve by telling lies, than with the shallower truth called factuality'.[10] In a more recent Burgess novel one character says of another (also a writer), 'He served the truth through a lying medium.'[11]

The Christian communicator can lie for the Lord's sake, lie for truth's sake, but he and his hearers must know what he is doing. What he must not do, even with the worthiest of pious motives, is deceive for the Lord's sake. Such deceptions can acquire in time the force of a different kind of narrative and so become vehicles of error rather than truth. Legend should be kept in its proper place. In Rome I have heard the *Quo Vadis* story attributed to the New Testament, and in Jerusalem I have heard the Veronica story attributed to the New Testament. Legend all too readily introduces itself into a different kind of narrative and claims a kind of truth to which it is not entitled, but in its proper place it can add colour and music to good narrative theology.

Parable

An American who specializes in the writing of modern parables has said that the characteristic feature of a parable is that it blows up in your face. That was certainly the experience of David on hearing Nathan's parable of the one ewe lamb. Such a parable leads you happily along inviting you to pass judgment on the characters in the story until the denouement reveals that you have passed judgment on yourself. To quote Sallie McFague again: 'The parable does not teach a spectator a lesson; rather it invites and surprises a participant into an experience.'[12] If that were not so, a parable would have done for us all it can do once we had heard it and noted its moral. In fact a parable can be read or heard over and over again without ceasing to do its work on us. As Sallie McFague goes on to say, 'This is its power, its power then and now to be revelatory, not once upon a time, but every time a person becomes caught up in it and by it.' She is herself one of those who treat the parable as an extended metaphor and therefore as a story which brings together the two interlocked worlds of time and eternity.

> The world of the parable . . . includes, it *is* both dimensions – the secular and the religious, our world and God's love. It is not that the parable points to the unfamiliar but that it includes the unfamiliar within its boundaries. The unfamiliar (the kingdom of God) is the context, the interpretative framework, for understanding life in this world. We are not taken out of this world when we enter the world of the parable, but we find ourselves in a world that is itself two-dimensional, a world in which the 'religious' dimension comes to the 'secular' and re-forms it.[13]

Sallie McFague speaks of Jesus as himself the metaphor of God, and Amos Wilder also finds Jesus' way of using parables to be deeply harmonious with his own nature.

> Without going into comparisons, we can say that in the parables of Jesus men come before us in their moral mystery and in a perspective of divine severity and love. But what is *sui generis* is the way in which these deeper dimensions are married to such ordinariness and secularity. The deepest mysteries of providence and destiny are at home with this naturalness. Here we have in Jesus' sayings the counterpart of his own person and presence among men: not as a philosopher, priest, or scribe, but as an artisan; not in the desert or in the temple, but in the market-place.[14]

He also regards the hearing of a true parable as a revelatory experience rather than a piece of instruction.

> As with a poem, the parable form as a distinctive kind of voice,

and by its architecture, reveals rather than persuades. So far as
it persuades, it is not by an induction, but by a visionary
recognition.[15]

'The stories', Wilder says, 'are so told as to compel men to see
things as they are.'[16]

If things as they are provide the stuff of parables, it should be
possible to go on making new ones out of things as they have now
come to be. Most of those who attempt it, however, seem to end
up with little more than a cautionary tale or a morality story. The
true parable must surely be the subtlest of all story forms. I have
leaned heavily on quotations even to describe its role as a communicator. I have nothing to offer on how to make modern
parables, but it is a job I long to see done.

The modernizing of classic parables is a job not quite so
demanding and has sometimes been done quite well. Some years
ago the *Hippity Dog* audio-visual strips issued by the Pastoral Aid
Society re-told some of the parables of Jesus with cartoon-type
animals taking all the parts. The parable of the pearl of great price
came out as the story of a retired military animal who sold everything – not only his golf clubs but his clothes – in order to buy
the star footballer needed by his local team.

To me this kind of whole-hog approach is more acceptable than
a cautious up-dating of incidental details. I have heard the parable
of the wise and the foolish virgins told in such a way that the
wedding was retained, the delayed bridegroom was retained, the
oil lamps were retained, but when the foolish virgins ran out of
oil they 'went off to the local Woolies to buy more'. This seems
to me to mix two different cultures in a way which robs both of
their reality.

Admittedly it may not be enough simply to repeat the story in
its New Testament form with nothing to bridge the first century
and the twentieth. It may be, however, that the most effective
bridge is that which leads the twentieth-century hearer back to
stand in the shoes of his or her first-century predecessor. Before
identifying with any character in such a story we probably need
to identify with those who first heard it. Standing on the common
ground we share with them we can enter their experience and

find that the parable illuminates in a lightning flash not only things as they were but things as they are.

To experience the force of the parable of the labourers in the vineyard it is not always necessary to have it re-told in terms of present-day union rules and shop stewards' reactions. If the story is left in its original form, however, the twentieth-century hearer must be led to feel his or her own kinship with the first hearers' sense of fair play, his or her own kinship with their feeling of having been for generations the Lord's people doing the Lord's work in a hostile environment. As the story proceeds we of the twentieth century can easily share, over and over again, the shock of discovering that in the eyes of Jesus we inhabit a world which simply is not a meritocracy. A world ruled by grace is still so surprising a discovery that we are likely to make it most often through the parable as used by Jesus.

Allegory

This chapter started with a sort of allegory from Theodore Roszak. Various details in the story of those frogs in the well answered to different aspects of human history. In allegory quite minor details have a significance which they do not have in parable. As John Bunyan showed – and not only in *Pilgrim's Progress* – the result can be persuasive as well as entertaining, moving and beautiful as well as true.

Its relation to truth is, however, a very distinctive one. The parable works because that is how things are. It is self-authenticating. Its effect is evidence of its truth. An allegory, however, rarely provides any reason why we should believe what it affirms. If we find it to be a vehicle of truth it is because we have found the evidence elsewhere. It can make a truth interesting, it can make the implications of that truth a lot clearer, it can make the whole affirmation moving and beautiful, but it cannot authenticate it. A group to which I gave the Theodore Roszak story decided as an exercise to re-write it because they found its message too depressing. They ended up with another charming frog story communicating an almost opposite conviction. Which of them was true had to be decided on grounds exterior to the story.

The danger of the allegory, then, is that it is almost too flexible a means of communication. It can hold and persuade by its own intrinsic charm, but the conviction which it communicates may be true or false. The classic *Everyman*, for instance, is surely an instrument of Pelagianism rather than of salvation by faith. Grace is involved but Good Works is Everyman's lasting helper. The allegory-maker has to be a specially disciplined story-teller: one who will not let the enjoyment of the narrative obscure the truth it is designed to serve.

For all that, the allegory-maker is still with us – and welcome. In 1974 in England Robert Way produced an elaborately detailed story of a garden and made it an allegory of Christian disciple-ship.[17] At about the same time in America Calvin Miller was making a verse allegory of the life of Christ through the figure of a singer.[18] Neither story has quite the independent story-line of Bunyan's classics, but each re-tells a familiar story with new symbols and images to exhibit its meaning and its beauty.

Illustration

Some stories, without being allegories, serve also to make a truth clearer and more attractive but without providing any reason for believing it. This is because the story bears no intrinsic relation-ship to that truth. The connection is manufactured by the story-teller. That is what I mean by an illustration. The communicator's skill and imagination link it to what is being affirmed and the receiver of the communication has every reason to be grateful. The point is made clearer and the hearing of it made pleasanter. It does not, however, point to a place where the two dimensions of which it speaks are actually joined to each other in reality.

For instance, Alasdair Heron speaks of a telling illustration used by Karl Barth.

> The appearance of the first, and the second, editions of *Romans* made a considerable and widespread impression. Barth himself later said that he had been like a man who, tripping in the darkness of the church tower, had accidentally caught hold of the bell-rope to steady himself and alarmed the whole country-side.[19]

Obviously there is no intrinsic connection between publishing a commentary and tripping over a bell-rope, but the illustration serves to describe what happened in a very vivid way. The image is memorable, but it is not evidence.

Communicators often treat illustrations and examples (see below) as the same thing, and the recipients of communication can be beguiled into thinking that a point well illustrated is a point made. Neither is the case. Illustrations are to be sought with zeal and enjoyed with relish, but not credited with an authority they do not possess.

I sometimes use an illustration from television in order to clarify what I want to say about the reading of the Bible. I talk about the device of superimposition. With electronic cameras and a standard mixer it is a simple matter to put the output of two cameras on the screen at the same time. Move each fader half way and you have the two pictures superimposed on each other. The result can be a mess, but done with care it can be illuminating. A singer can be shown in big close-up to reveal minute facial expressions and at the same time in long-shot to reveal bodily stance and gesture. Or an object can be examined from two different angles at the same time. In each case the simultaneity of the perception can add something to the more normal experience of seeing things one at a time and adding up impressions afterwards.

In a somewhat similar way our everyday view of the world and the biblical view of the world should be examined, I would say, simultaneously. The one picture should be mentally superimposed on the other. It is not enough to turn from one to the other and try to work out connections. We need to see our own immediate environment through the superimposed picture of the world as the Bible reveals it, and we need to see the biblical world through the superimposed picture of our own experience. It is a matter less of exposition than of perception. We need to *see* biblically.

The illustration from television technology helps, I hope, to make clearer what I am getting at, but I then have to offer some evidence that what I am saying is true and that what I am recommending does actually prove effective. To do that I would have to provide not illustrations but examples.

Example

A story which showed a truth being applied and tested would constitute evidence in support of that truth, and in my system of labelling it would be an example rather than an illustration. We are really back in the realms of documentary, but I am thinking now of the particular and individual experience rather than of salvation history as a whole.

Perversely perhaps, I want to include in this category stories which are pure fiction. Of course they must be presented as the fictions they are, but one way to get people to examine the truth in their own experience and to look for examples within their own experience is to present them with a fictional embodiment of that truth and ask them to consider whether it is plausible. 'This did not happen, but do you think it could have done? Are these ficticious characters behaving and reacting in a way which at all answers to your own experience?' The ficticious example of a truth applied becomes the model of a true example.

For instance (and an instance is, after all, an example), in *The Birds Fall Down* by Rebecca West a Russian in Paris who is in principle a terrorist and in practice a sensitive and compassionate individual becomes convinced that it is his duty to kill a man of whom he is convinced that he has betrayed both revolutionaries and Czarists. With his finger on the trigger he discovers that the suspect is blind and therefore could not be guilty. They talk, and a character of exceptional goodness and simplicity is revealed in the man who was to have been murdered.

> I didn't think, as you might expect, 'How guilty I am for having tried to kill this innocent man'. I thought simply, 'That is an innocent man', and I became fixed in contemplation of him, like a compass pointing to the North. It was as if what he was, the pure substance of him, wiped out my offence against him. I understood for the first time what is meant by the forgiveness of sins.[20]

The fictional story prompts practical questions. Could such an experience lead to an understanding of what is meant by the forgiveness of sins? Does the contemplation of innocence – the reality, not the fiction – cause us to reorientate ourselves like a compass swinging to the north? In that position does the 'pure substance' of the Innocent wipe out our offence? The ficticious example sends us hunting through our own experience for parallels: the crucified Christ readily takes the place of the blind man and the doctrine of the forgiveness of sins is not merely illustrated but found to be grounded in actual evidence of the way in which human nature operates.

As always, however, the story has to be looked through and not merely at. This applies to every category of narrative listed in this chapter. We have to ask not just Did it happen? but What does it mean? All experiences, and therefore all narratives, are mirrors of truth, symbols which have to be interpreted. That, as we have seen, is not the twentieth-century way. So the story-teller has to be sure to tell his tale in such a way that it demands interpretation – and demands the *kind* of interpretation proper to the kind of story that it is.

Only then will the story affect both mind and imagination, invade the territories occupied in our time by the warring armies of fact and fantasy. We have seen a little of the way in which human conduct can be shaped by mental images. These images are themselves shaped by stories. 'Every story', the old adage *might* have said, 'tells a picture.'

5

Pictures

At a local church's weekend conference we were discussing how we could chat to a neighbour in a bus queue or over a garden fence in such a way that something of our faith would be communicated without our sounding like propagandists or recruiting sergeants – with all the negative results which would follow from that. We ended up with the formula 'Don't tell them what they should believe, show them what you see.'

To reveal the world as the Christian sees it is to begin the communication process at the beginning. It establishes the context within which dialogue can take place. Often it reveals what the dialogue should be about in so far as any conversation may reveal two quite different ways of seeing what is there in the world, and two quite different ways of reacting to what is seen. The Christian perception involves not only a grateful way of looking at the world's beauty, but a compassionate way of looking at the world's sorrows and a committed way of looking at both. The Christian sees the world as something he or she is united with and is required both to affirm and redeem. It is the meeting place of two orders of reality, one spiritual and one material. To look at it that way is to see something quite different from what is seen when it is looked at as just a material environment from which each must wrest such security and pleasure as can be had. The second view is challenged first of all by letting emerge a description of the way things look from the other standpoint.

Elements of such a description can be embodied with perfect naturalness in chat about work, sport, gardening or community.

To the Christian all are parts of a whole which is characterized by purpose, and all are parts of a whole which is an image of glory. Not only in communication but in personal experience the perception is prior to the precept. We act as we do because we see things as we do. We believe what we believe because that belief answers to our images of life. I must quote George Caird again.

> Belief in God depends to a small extent on rational argument, and to a larger extent on our ability to frame images to capture, commemorate and convey our experience of transcendence.[1]

Such images can be presented verbally or visually, but either way the image-making process depends on a particular understanding of the way the world is and of how it relates to God. There are two classical and obvious mistakes to be made. One is to suppose that an image *is* divine or contains the divine, the other is to suppose that no image can in any way express or relate to divinity.

Israel of old was surrounded by nations which treated their graven images as themselves gods. It was against this background that the Hebrew scriptures forbade all visual representations of the deity – a prohibition which carried over into Islam and into the iconoclastic movements within Christianity. It constitutes a necessary warning against treating an image as anything *more* than an image. An image is, in this context, just a mirror catching one stray beam of eternal light, a pointer directing attention away from itself in isolation to that which contains it and transcends it. To accord an artefact greater significance than that is idolatry. To accord the universe greater significance than that is pantheism. God remains the Other. He must not be confused with any of the visible things which imperfectly reflect his being.

In the end, however, since words also paint pictures, the denial of all images would make God unknowable, inexpressible, incommunicable. No kind of relationship with him would be possible. In fact the Old Testament is full of verbal images of God: he is rock, he is fire, he is a fortress. His wisdom is a woman of great beauty. His human creatures, all the children of Noah, are bearers of his image. His creation bears the stamp of his Word. Job says 'But now mine eye seeth thee' (Job 42.5), but it does no such thing. There is no theophany in the book of Job. Job's vision consists of a fresh look at the world and its inhabitants. His eye has seen not God, but a series of images of divine power and mystery.

Certainly the world as we know it is a very imperfect mirror of the divine, and human nature as we have it is a spoiled image of God. But the relationship between God and humanity, God and the world, is never denied in the Bible. Irenaeus suggested that man was created 'in the image and likeness of God' and that he has destroyed the likeness but retains the image.

The New Testament affirms that the clear image and likeness are to be seen in Christ, that the divine has been expressed in what eyes have seen, ears have heard and hands have handled. And if the physical Christ is that kind of image of God, then all flesh and blood, all soil and substance, are capable of double significance – the double significance which Jesus himself found in the flowers of the field, the birds of the air, the child in the midst. Nothing is itself alone. It is a particular junction between creation and creator, between time and eternity. As Traherne said of his own childhood, 'Something infinite behind everything appeared.'[2]

Not everybody lives as if inhabiting such a world. In Charles Causley's *Collected Poems* is one called 'At Kfar Kana'. It tells of an incident which took place on a package tour in Israel. The bus disgorged its passengers at yet another allegedly authenticated site of a famous miracle. Causley wandered off alone and, while his fellow passengers inspected the inevitable church and purchased the inevitable souvenirs, he watched two children playing at a well. They brought him bright water in a paper cup and reminded him where he was: Kfar Kana, Cana of Galilee. To other members of the party it was the place where 'a far, famous act' may have been performed, and where they obtained a particular piece of embroidered cloth or hammered brass. To Causley it was the place

> Where children changed for me
> Well-water into wine.[3]

Many tourists and pilgrims reach back to a point in time or a place in geography and let their attention rest there. The poet reaches through that moment and location to that which transcends time and space. In both cases there is a visual experience. In one case the mind rests on the given object, past or present. In the other case the visual experience is one in which the eye finds a living image capable of joining past and present, heaven and earth. It is the difference between a world of sights and a world of symbols. We have to learn from artists of all sorts – poets, painters, prophets and many others – to look *at* and to look *through*, to see things as they are but also for what they are in the perspective of eternity and as images of glory.

The visitor to holy places is inevitably in danger of seeking to know Christ 'after the flesh', as Paul says in II Corinthians 5.16. Given our incarnational faith it is, as far as it goes, a valid desire. But we do not know Christ until his physicality has become an image of his eternal nature. Inviting children always and only to make the approach of the hymn which says 'I should like to have been with them then' may be to encourage the development of single vision instead of the double vision which is needed.

Recently in several churches (because of their using the same admirable scheme of teaching) I have seen delightful evidence of children's work on 'what life was like in the time of Jesus'. In one place I even saw the children making bread in the way a first-century Jew would make it so that they could share with their tongues in the actual taste which Jesus knew. It was splendid. But I wonder if they were any nearer at the end to what Jesus meant when he spoke of bread as a symbol of himself. Given good teaching alongside the action they probably were, but it is not difficult for a preoccupation with the actual to get in the way of the symbolic.

Neither with children nor with adults is it enough to get people back to the circumstances surrounding the first communication of the Christian gospel. Having reached that point we have then to *receive* the communication, and that means seeing images and not just sights. As H. Richard Niebuhr said, 'One must look with Paul and the evangelists, not at them.'[4] Niebuhr speaks in terms of seeing, and that is right. It is not just a matter of receiving what the apostles taught when they had seen what they saw, but of seeing with them and of perceiving the significance of what passed before their eyes.

I am reminded of an image used years ago in the course of a theological lecture by a greatly respected biblical scholar. He described the experience of reading the Bible as like that of two young men walking along a street in the wake of a girl. 'That', says one of them, 'is a very attractive girl.'

'How do you know?', says the other. 'We haven't seen her face.'

'No, but we've seen the faces of people coming towards us. They *have* seen it.'

That sort of indirect, reflected vision is, I was told, all that is available to us. But it is enough. More might well be too much for us. Where the divine glory is concerned, to see it reflected in the testimony of witnesses may be as much as we can yet bear. But it must be *seeing*. We have to look with them not at them. We have to try and capture through the reflection in their eyes, through the impact on their minds, through the response of their lives, what it was that they saw – and what it was that they saw in and through what was visible to them. We then have to turn to our own world and see it in that reflected light.

To content ourselves with their words as if the vision were captured in verbal formulas and intellectual concepts may be one form of that literalism which we have already noticed as a present-day characteristic. We have to go through the words to the picture, and through the picture to what lies beyond it and within it. The picture which only denotes a visible reality may illustrate Christian truth, but to become itself an experience of that truth it has also to express the invisible, to join the two worlds of God's kingdom and men's experience. The true image is derived from the world which meets the eye but is also a projection of what is inward and a reflection of what is eternal.

Graphic images

'Graphic' may not be quite the correct term, but I intend this section to be about visual images expressed visually, as distinct from visual images expressed through the medium of words. Here we are concerned with pictures as language, later with language as pictures.

As far as non-verbal images are concerned it is natural that a disciple of Blake (the great enemy of 'single vision') should show us the way. Samuel Palmer was Blake's younger contemporary and said

> Creation sometimes pours into the spiritual eye the radiance of heaven: the green mountains . . . the moon . . . not only thrill the optic nerve, but shed an unearthly lustre into the inmost spirits, and seem the intruding twilight of that peaceful country, where there is no sorrow and no night. . . . I cannot think it other than the veil of heaven . . . and proscenium of eternity.[5]

Moved by this belief he settled in Shoreham – Shoreham in Kent, not the seaside one – and for a time poured out pictures which were clearly accounts of that particular countryside and yet were simultaneously visions of a world caught up into a heavenly peace. They look somehow biblical in spite of being visibly English.

Another way of joining past and present via the transcendant is that of Sir Stanley Spencer. His very stylized and sometimes grotesque figures are not to everyone's taste as representations of Christ and his apostles, but it is not inappropriate to depict such characters in a way which sets them a little apart from the styles and shapes of any particular period, and it was entirely natural to Spencer to paint the New Testament story as taking place in his own riverside village of Cookham. To him Cookham was 'possessed of a sacred presence'. Sir John Rothenstein quotes this phrase and speaks of Spencer's 'simultaneous dual vision of Cookham people and happenings and of Bible stories'.[6] It was characteristic of this way of seeing the world that he could say 'all ordinary acts such as the sewing on of a button are religious things and a part of perfection'. It was a pity that he could not consistently see his wife's ordinary acts in this way, but it is that perception of the sacredness of the ordinary which made it possible to see the gospel story taking place in Cookham and which gives rise to parables and to images. Palmer and Spencer both in a sense (and in very different ways) painted visions of the biblical world and of the familiar world with the one superimposed on the other and yet integrated with it.

Since so much of modern communication comes in the form of pictures on a screen, and since the Christian faith is communicated by narrative and description, we cannot afford to ignore the visual expression of our faith. Often we confess that faith (or deny it) visually without even knowing that we are doing so. Body language, for instance, is a form of visual communication. The forced smile no less than the sulky glare delivers a message – one which is often received with more sensitivity and accuracy than verbal messages are.

Not only bodies but buildings speak. The psalmist may have said that 'in his temple doth every one (or every thing) speak of his glory' (Ps. 29.9), but this is unfortunately not true of all temples and churches. Some buildings speak of human pretentiousness, some hark back to the days of great public meetings and some to days of priestly remoteness and separation from the people. A liturgical revolution has moved altars and changed the position of celebrants all over the world in the last thirty years or so precisely because the old arrangements were not saying visually what Christians now want to say. Whether every member of a congregation could explain in words just what the changes signified is extremely doubtful, but that does not mean that people were unaffected by them or did not get the message. Visual impressions reach to parts of the personality unplumbed by words.

But the task which largely remains to be done is that of framing images in which people can see the contemporary world and the eternal at one. Sometimes this has to be done by using words to delineate one half of the equation and matching the words with pictures which speak of the other half. The devotional television programme *This is the Day* has been running, on and off, for some years now. It has always had two or three biblical readings, but the words have always been accompanied by films or photographs of the present day world. It is not easy to achieve the right match between the two. Sometimes the pictures are so obvious a counterpart of the words (modern fishing boats when Galileean fishermen are mentioned) that they constitute little more than illustrations;

sometimes the gap between word and picture is so wide (a modern newsroom to go with readings about the signs of the times) that it takes some mental gymnastics to work out the connection. Much of the time, however, words and images come as two parts of a single experience which neither of them alone could communicate. They are not joined in the head by subsequent thought, but the two senses of seeing and hearing receive them as a single communication in which the biblical world and the present world are linked by their common relationship to the transcendent.

Visual language, moreover, has better claims to being classless, ageless, universal than any verbal language has. Ask the members of any group to jot down a suggestion for a visual image of purity, and you will get not only very similar images all round the group but also a very similar range of images whatever the age or social characteristics of any other group you try it with. It would be interesting to extend the experiment in other countries and other cultures to see to what extent the visual image transcends the differences.

The message communicated by a visual image is, however, another example of a signal which can by-pass the critical faculties and the awareness of the recipient. Photograph an unshaven male face from below and it will look threatening. Photograph the same face from above and it will look pitiful. Yet few will realize that the message has been determined by the photographer rather than by the object. Not for nothing does the housewife in the television commercial look up to a high camera when answering the questions of her unseen interlocutor. It is all part of the intended little-woman image. Not for nothing is the beer drinker in a brewer's advertisement shot from a waist-high camera position. His being seen against ceiling or against sky is all part of the intended macho image.

Christian communicators should not be eager to participate in image-making of this synthetic kind, but they do have a view of the world to communicate and it cannot all be done verbally. The television way of matching traditional words with contemporary pictures is available to any church with projection facilities. Not religious art but pictures of what lies outside the church doors and in the afflicted parts of the earth are what do most to combine word and picture into a religious image. Better still, the church group with video facilities can both make and use meditations which combine word, music and picture in one multi-dimensional experience.

The technology is not the problem. The real difficulty is our inexperience with images which project the result of Christian dual vision. What we are accustomed to seeing on the screen, even when it is symbolic (like the unshaven face), is often designed to suggest that whatever fears or aspirations are aroused in us there is a material (and probably purchasable) way of dealing with them. Here is another story from a different book by Theodore Roszak. This time it belongs as story to the category of example and not allegory, but its subject is the image.

The musical accompaniment is by Richard Strauss: *Also Sprach Zarathustra*. Over it, a portentous voice announces, 'From the beginning of time, man has dreamed of one supreme adventure: to traverse the heavens with the grace of a bird.'

And now, a bird appears before us, neatly sailing the wind. From below, a man gazes up, his face filled with fascination and longing. He is shaggy, covered in animal hides . . . a stereo-typic caveman. But he has fashioned himself a pair of outsized wings. He ties them on and steps to the edge of a dizzy preci-pice. And then, as his troglodytic colleagues stand by in awed amazement, the original aviator spreads his wings and soars away into the sun . . . only to be transformed in midair into a Boeing 707, the *true* 'wings of man'.

It is a television commercial for a prominent American air-line, a slick, pretentious spot announcement that finished by reminding how all of us can enjoy the 'supreme adventure' for as little as $214 Los Angeles to Atlanta round trip, Mondays through Thursdays, economy fare.

I watch and ponder the wealth of artistic and religious symbol-ism that lies hidden beneath this popular, potted history of avia-tion. Classic images of flight and ascendance fill my thoughts . . . and I grow sad to see a noble imagery debased to the level of so poor a counterfeit . . .

Yet how *could* so great and ancient a dream turn out to be so trivial? . . . We must recognize that somewhere along the line we have lost touch with the traditional aspiration. We have made it real – materially, historically real – but at the expense of some other, greater reality . . . something that eludes us for all our power and cunning.[7]

It can happen, but it does not *have* to happen. A television image such as the flight of a bird can still be made to arouse expectations and aspirations which no marketable commodity can satisfy. When the prophet says 'You shall mount up with wings as eagles' he is using picture language which no amount of aviation can prevent from getting inside us and kindling hopes which have nothing to do with hang-gliding. He, however, is using *verbal* imagery.

Verbal images

These simply paint their pictures on the mind without the use of the graphic arts, but they remain pictures and are subject to the same laws as the visible ones. The classic examples are to be found in John's Gospel in the 'I am' sayings of Jesus: 'I am the door . . . the bread . . . the light . . . the shepherd . . .' and so on. These are clearly pictorial expressions, and clearly also symbolic ones. Literalism in the reading of picture language causes as much trouble as in other fields. Those who wish to justify a once standard view of what happens at the eucharist are still sometimes heard to declare 'Jesus said "This is my body" and I believe him.' Nobody would ask them to *dis*-believe him, but it is important to understand the way in which he used words and images. The sort of literalism which gave us the cruder forms of the doctrine of transubstantiation could set us looking for hinges in the one who said 'I am the door.' Clearly the picture language of Old and New Testaments is not that kind of language. It is the language of a people to whom all pictures are symbols because to them the whole world was a world of images.

When their language came to be understood as verbally exact, the impossible implications were for centuries dissolved away by a typological method of interpretation. Symbolism was reimposed on the texts by means of a sort of second-generation set of symbols. Sometimes, though, the original symbolic and imagistic idiom was retained and was allowed to extend itself in verbal images of the same character. At the roots of our British Christian tradition is a Celtic strand which retained better than the Latin strand did the graphic tangibleness of the biblical image, and much of this was carried over into Anglo-Saxon.

The Dream of the Rood, for instance, re-tells the crucifixion story in terms of a dream or vision in which an ornate crucifix becomes the true cross, and that cross speaks to tell its story in words which can all be *seen* – or rather, in words which are hardly noticed because the pictures they paint are so vivid that the mind is preoccupied with looking.

> Then I saw the King   of all mankind
> In brave mood hasting   to mount upon me.
> Refuse I dared not,   nor bow nor break,
> Though I felt earth's confines   shudder in fear;
> All foes I might fell,   yet still I stood fast.
> Then the young Warrior,   God the All-Wielder,
> Put off His raiment,   steadfast and strong;
> With lordly mood   in the sight of many
> He mounted the Cross   to redeem mankind.[8]

(In this version by Charles W. Kennedy there is a pause in the middle of each line because he seeks to preserve the rhythm, as he does the alliteration, of the original.)

This is very much the language of the tradition which Jesus inherited, as witness the apocryphal book of the Wisdom of Solomon: 'All things were lying in peace and silence, and night in her swift course was half spent, when thy almighty Word leapt from thy royal throne in heaven into the midst of that doomed land like a relentless warrior, bearing the sharp sword of thy inflexible decree' (18.14–16, NEB).

This is a theological style which might have come back in the twentieth century after the publication in 1931 of Gustaf Aulen's *Christus Victor*, but in fact the language of Christian testimony still seems relatively pale. This applies equally to evangelicals calling for a standardized religious experience and using standardized terminology to evoke it, to the socially concerned radicals expounding the case for international initiatives in the language style of a newspaper editorial, to the pastoral-psychological types offering counsel and help in a language derived from a blending of psychology and sociology. All are capable of adding emphasis by raising their voices and all may be serving the truth, but few are making their authority *visible*. There is a lack of self-authenticating imagery. It is not just a matter of making our prosaic utterances more poetic or more forceful, but of making the shared experience more of a perception and less of a precept or concept. We need to paint pictures, and they need to be pictures which are inherently symbolic so that they can be seen *through* and thus acquire the mystical force of the biblical image.

As with metaphor, it will be useful to distinguish between the making of new images and the refreshing of old ones.

To discover a powerful image – and it is again discovery not invention, because the connection between the image and what is reflected in it is an intrinsic connection, not an artificial one – it is first of all necessary to live where, as Traherne also said of his childhood, 'eternity was manifest in the light of day'. Given some degree of inner stillness in such a situation things do light up with fresh significance, and given some skill with words the vision can be communicated by simple description. It is not at all a blossoming of flowery language that is called for, but a holding of the image long enough and quietly enough for the receiver of the communication to look at it and through it. In spoken communication it is particularly important to give time for the image to be contemplated. In writing, since the pace is set by the reader, images can be touched in more lightly.

Richard Holloway finds a fragment of such language in a novel by Evelyn Waugh, but in introducing it he himself develops some strong images pointing to the kind of experience out of which strong images come. He is speaking of 'the difference between the magnificence of our longing and the mediocracy of our lives' and says of man:

Even his most wonderful discoveries in art and his deepest experiences of love are, finally, unable to bear the full weight of his longing. What he is looking for is never completely within them, it only shines through them, tantalizing him again to continue the search for the light that never was on sea or land. All we get are glimpses, now and then, of the shadow which turns the corner always a pace or two ahead of us. In *Brideshead Revisited*, Evelyn Waugh caught the transient, wistful quality of all our earthly loves: 'Perhaps all our loves are merely hints and symbols; vagabond language scrawled on gate-posts and paving-stones along the weary road that others have tramped before us . . .'⁹

Fragile as all images are rightly there said to be, such language works memorably.

As to the refreshing of old images, time and concentration are even more necessary. It is very much the same process as that already described for the bringing to life of dead metaphors. People who take their language from the Bible are bound to use visual imagery, but they can scatter images like confetti so that they fall on the mind as so many cliches. An image from the past has to be looked at afresh and given time to reflect its inner light. 'With thee is the fountain of life', says the psalmist (Ps. 36.9). 'A fountain of life', says the preacher, and rushes on as if the words had the same kind of obviousness as 'Pass the marmalade'. Before the paragraph is ended he may well have thrown in three other biblical images (the wind of the spirit, the bread of life, the shield of faith), a couple of modern ones (a green light, a traffic jam) and a few timeless ones (an open door, calm waters, the light of truth).

We tend to use picture language as just colouring material to adorn an utterance which would otherwise be penny-plain. We need to let an image establish its own relationship to truth and communicate for itself, but we rather assume that the truth is actually to be found in our own argument and that we are only colouring it in for the sake of rhetoric.

The preacher needs to stay with that fountain and let it play on the imagination. At the preparatory stage he could have made himself look at it. He could offer to his imagination a particular fountain, set in a possible environment – perhaps a hot and dusty one. In his mind he could watch the light on the springing waters. He could see the fountain refresh the ground and cool the air. He could watch life gather about it and draw on it. He could see it as an instrument of cleansing and a cause of growth. He would not need to give a separate meaning to each detail as if he were composing an allegory, but he would allow the complete image to display its visual power and to reflect that other light of which it is a picture – and of which it is a picture not because literary artifice has made it so, but because that is what it *is* in the nature of the created order and its relationship to God.

Then when he comes to pass on the message, the preacher must give his hearers a chance to share the experience by giving them time to *see* the fountain and to contemplate it as a significant image. The psalmist may have been able (in the interests of Hebraic parallelism) to pass straight on from the image of the fountain to the image of light, but the modern congregation is accustomed to using language differently and cannot read visual signals at all rapidly. In time, though, the image of the fountain does blend naturally into the image of light.

It is a little odd that a generation which has grown up to hours of viewing pictures on a television screen appears to have emerged from the process in some danger of being visually illiterate (see chapter 9). Certainly there are some young people who show a highly sophisticated sensitivity to the quality of the sounds in recorded music and yet have never noticed that there is a sort of visual grammar which governs the way pictures are joined together in a film or television sequence. Along with this goes a visual equivalent of being tongue-tied when it come to framing significant images either graphically or in words. Perhaps it is due to their having been brought up on images which were either (as with cartoons) so unrealistic as to occupy only the world of fantasy, or else so documentary-realistic as to lack all significance as symbolism. The skill we have to learn is that of joining the immanent and the transcendent in the perception of the visible.

Today's preference for bare statement in matters of religion is not merely aesthetic. We are less and less at home in the language of symbols and images. Our bent, technological rather than scientific, makes us naive and literal, so that we often confuse the symbol with the thing it symbolizes; and there is no surer way than this of robbing a symbol of vital significance.[10]

This warning by the Bishop of Winchester needs to be taken with particular seriousness when we are using picture language – or, indeed, pictures. Literalism can reduce the greatest of images to the status of mere illustrations. They adorn or prettify a text, but do not themselves communicate its meaning. Yet the twentieth-century mind of full of meaningful images – bearers of a quite inadequate interpretation of the reality around us. The need is for truer and more vivid descriptions of that reality. 'Show them what you *see*.'

6

Dialogue

'Most spoken communication is dialogue even when it's monologue.' I occasionally allow myself this paradox (or worse) because
I find that the monologue which means most to me as a recipient
of communication is the one which engages in implicit dialogue
with my unspoken thoughts. The speaker makes a point. I think of
an objection. He meets precisely that objection, almost as if he
had heard me. My mind says 'Yes, but . . .' He deals with my
'but'.

He does all the speaking, but he has listened to my point of
view – probably in others rather than in me. He has faced up
to my questions and is meeting my difficulties. He shows – what
we saw in chapter 1 to be essential – an understanding of the
recipient of the communication. And that understanding cannot be had on the cheap. The good communicator is a good
listener. He has really to have attended to the difficulties in the
way of his affirmation. He has to have felt their force for himself
or he will not engage effectively in that implicit dialogue with
me.

I want to say something about implicit dialogue, about explicit
dialogue and about dramatic dialogue, but most important of all
is this basic attitude to dialogue itself. The Christian communicator naturally and rightly feels that he has a message. He less
rightly is inclined to assume that his task is to concentrate on that
message and not divert his attention to take in the idle dreams,
the fantasies, the hopes, the fears, the difficulties of those to
whom he is sent. Like Moses, he comes down from the mountain

with the truth engraved on tablets of stone. Others may take it or leave it.

But he is not like Moses. Only Moses is like Moses. And even in the Bible the truth is more often discovered in the course of dialogue than it is handed down in tablet form. Dialogue is necessary to the communicator not only as a means of passing on the truth but as a means of finding it out. The Old Testament shows men wrestling with each other in order to possess the truth, and wrestling with God too. Jacob becomes Israel in the course of wrestling at the ford Jabbok (Gen. 24.24–31). Earlier in Genesis, Abraham has argued with God in a dialogue in which for all his deference Abraham argues relentlessly and wins a number of concessions (Gen. 18.22–23). Later we find prophets challenging accepted views and pushing us on towards a truth larger than either of the positions stated with (apparently) divine authority. Thus Ezekiel's insistence that the innocent son of a guilty father does not suffer for his father's sins (Ezek. 18.14–17) is not to be easily reconciled with the assertion of the decalogue: 'I the Lord thy God am a jealous God, visiting the iniquity of the fathers upon the children unto the third and fourth generation of them that hate me' (Ex. 20.5). The two affirmations both stand, and truth is to be found through the tension between them rather than by a bland endorsement of either.

The prophetic cry of 'Thus saith the Lord' does not seem to mean 'The statement which follows has been dictated to me and must be accepted as verbally exact.' It means 'God has shown me what he is doing through current events: listen and I will communicate their significance to you.' What then follows is an utterance in the distinct style of a particular prophet. There is no mistaking Ezekiel for Jeremiah, or either of them for Amos. The utterance of a Greek oracle might be regarded as verbally divine (though interpretation could give it almost any meaning), but the Hebrew tradition was different. There it was rather the meaning that was divinely revealed and the prophet then communicated it through every medium his culture provided and he could use. Often this meant using poetic language rather than prose, or symbolic story rather than commandment, or body language rather than words. Ezekiel played with two sticks in order to communicate on the subject of the divided kingdoms, Jeremiah buried his linen girdle under a rock and left it there to rot in order to communicate the fate of Jerusalem. Both of them were locked in dialogue with the people around them and framed their communications in such a way as to reach to the heart of the people with whom they argued.

In the New Testament, Jesus certainly speaks with authority, and he does not hesitate to command or to restate an ancient commandment. That is his right. But even he puts questions as well as answering them, engages in dialogue with both followers and opponents, and speaks in parables which only yield their meaning if the recipient participates actively in thinking about them. He does not pour his truth into empty vessels passively receiving it. He prompts people to grasp that truth by getting involved in the tension between that which is already known and that which is yet to be understood.

Paul in his letters reveals that there is dialogue going on within himself: 'I delight in the law of God after the inward man, but I see another law in my members, warring against the law of my mind' (Rom. 7.22f.); between himself and God: 'groanings which cannot be uttered' (Rom. 8.26); between himself and his correspondents: 'Now concerning the things whereof ye wrote unto me . . .' (I Cor. 7.1). He even makes an anxious distinction between answers on which he feels he has the word of Jesus, and answers for which he is dependent on his own submission to the Spirit of God: 'to the rest speak I, not the Lord . . .' (I Cor. 7.12). What is more, in order to communicate the truth which he has seen he will adapt himself to the needs of the recipient rather than insist on passing on his message just the way he received it himself: 'I am made all things to all men, that I might by all means save some' (I Cor. 9.22).

All of this seems a long way off from the painless assurance with which some modern communicators pass on their version of the truth, having received it in unstressful detachment from those to whom they hope to communicate it, and having discussed it only with those who are already like-minded. But the word of God is not a ready-made, handed down truth. There is indeed an unchanged and unchangeable core to it, and for that Moses' engraved stones might well be a symbol, but as a living word it is addressed to each hearer in a way conditioned by that hearer's needs and circumstances. It *is* a revelation from above and it *does* reach us through events in past history, but it is actually received with all the sharpness of a two-edged sword in the course of an encounter with the world, with its people and with the forces presently at work in ourselves as in others. 'Truth through tension' would be a slogan perfectly compatible with the nature of biblical revelation as the Bible itself describes the process. Our calling is not to inherit a reach-me-down version of what the biblical witnesses discovered but to join them in the struggle through which they discovered it.

> What is needed . . . in interpretation and preaching is not a return to allegory and typology but a faithful exegesis and exposition of Scripture that will wrestle with the words of these ancient witnesses until the walls of the centuries become thin and they tell us in *our* day what they knew so well in *their* day.[1]

But is not just a matter of getting freshly involved in wrestlings of long ago, as James D. Smart goes on to make clear. The dialogue has to be continued in the fresh terms set by modern experience and in the new media available as the contemporary arena. Dennis Nineham compares the interplay of past and present with the experience of a man who has learned much by living abroad but has now come home again.

> Suppose an Englishman goes to live for several years in Italy and finds the experience enjoyable and stimulating. He may come to speak Italian and to live, dress and feed after the Italian fashion. Supposing him to be a man of any sensitivity, we may be sure that if he eventually returns to live in England he will be a very different person from the man he was before he went. That does not mean that he will attempt to reproduce his Italian way of life on the English scene. If he is wise, he will not speak Italian all the time, eat exclusively Italian food, dress after the Italian manner or even adopt Italian attitudes to politics in the English political situation. When in England he will do as

England does, and the influence of the Italian experience will manifest itself in various differences *in his way of being English*, differences of which in some cases he will be aware, though in some cases they may be more apparent to others than they are to him.

It is in some such way as this that the influence of the . . . biblical beliefs and attitudes should be understood.[2]

What we need is a biblical way of being twentieth century, a way of discovering and communicating truth through a dialogue which is both ancient and modern.

Implicit dialogue

If a monologue speaker (such as a preacher) really knows and understands the generation he is addressing, the content of his exposition will be framed as a dialogue with what is going on in their minds. But it is not only a matter of content. The style of address also needs to be adjusted to the dialogue form through which they are accustomed to discover truth. When the public meeting and the printed word were the dominant forms of communication, people became accustomed to sustained exposure to a single point of view. No longer is that the case. The national leaders in politics and in general culture are now most often to be seen being interviewed, and the questions put to them (as we shall see) usually arise from a position which is different from, if not actively hostile to, that of the interviewee. Another major source of information and understanding is the television documentary. One feature of documentary is that it is built around a hard core of tangible, visible evidence – evidence interpreted in different ways by different contributors to the programme. Tension, dialogue and dialectic are the accepted modes of modern communication.

When people attend church they may put on different clothes mentally as well as physically, but if their day-to-day thinking and behaviour are going to be challenged and influenced, then the preacher must meet them on terms which are relevant to their day-to-day way of thinking and experiencing. The more that churches adopt a jargon and a communication style which is all their own, the more likely congregations are to pursue their week-day lives and thinking processes in a way which is little influenced by their Sunday churchgoing. This will be equally true – perhaps even more true – if they very greatly value and enjoy their weekly drawing apart into a different culture with its reassuring sense of belonging to a different and more favoured community.

It is possible that preachers could learn quite a bit from documentary producers – not necessarily about the content of their message, but about the type of presentation to which people are now responding. To begin with, a good documentary (unless it is just a general interest programme such as a nature film) is always answering a question. It may be the producer's own question or one that has been set for him, but it is the programme's business to press that one question on behalf of the whole viewing audience. A job to be done very early in the programme is to make clear what the issue is, and to make clear to viewers that it is a question of real importance to themselves. 'You need to know' is often the unspoken theme of the first sequence.

It would not be a bad beginning to a sermon either. There seems to be a lot of difference in the quality of the attention accorded when the preacher begins by giving the impression that he is going to try and answer a question which is real and important in the lives of the people in the pews, as distinct from the occasions when he or she appears to be talking in a way which is determined mainly by the fact that this *is* the way that talking is done on Sundays in churches. I have had occasion sometimes to be introduced as speaking on personal relationships and marital break-down. Unless I am mistaken, there is from the start a special kind of wary attentiveness on these occasions. Often it is doubtless due to a feeling that I may be skating on thin ice where particular families are concerned, but the fact that what I am going to be on about is known – and is known to be of present impor-tance – must contribute to it. Naturally, the fact that the question arises from the life of the world today does not prevent the answer from drawing on the biblical revelation and the classic tradition.

The producers of a television documentary have next to present the evidence they have assembled. And they probably do think of all their material as being evidence. There will be sequences indicating the nature of the problem as experienced by ordinary people: shots of houses or fields, factories or deserts; 'vox pops' from people at the heavy end of the issue. There will also be sequences in which official voices probably say that as much is being done as can be done, and unofficial voices that this is not the case. There will be sequences in which various experts analyse the situation in as dispassionate way as they can. All this is evidence, and all these people are witnesses. In the edited documentary each of them is likely to be called a number of times so that their contributions are set against each other in a way which constitutes a dialogue between them. If there is tension between the statements made by different contributors, those contributions are likely to be intercut very closely so that the tension is increased rather than diminished. The viewer should feel torn between the two. That is what offers the best chance that the issue will be seen in perspective.

It could be the same with the sermon. The preacher will have assembled relevant materials from a variety of sources: the Bible, Christian history, religious experience, news of the day. Each source can be thought of as a witness, and each witness can contribute some piece of hard evidence for an answer to the controlling question. What is more, the evidence can be presented in an order which is determined by the requirements of dramatic dialogue rather than in accord with some more academic pattern such as that of chronology. If there is tension between the witnesses – and there will be if the preacher has been listening to the dialogue rather than picking up packaged conclusions – then it could be brought out rather than played down. That text from Ezekiel and that contrasting commandment can be placed side by side rather than far apart. It would be more important for the congregation to feel the difficulty of reconciling individual responsibility with corporate involvement than it is to lead them smoothly along a route on which only one school of map-makers is allowed to erect signposts. The tension not only makes the talking more interesting but encourages the congregation to feel their way forward to a larger truth which must somehow embrace both the truths of the conflicting statements.

It also does something to meet a habit of the modern mind which many regard as a weakness but which does appear to exist and so has to be dealt with. I am referring to our much deplored inability to concentrate the mind in one direction for any length of time. A change of scene, a shift in point of view, an altered pace seem to be necessary if somnolence is not to take over. 'Nobody,' said a very intelligent and well-established church member, 'nobody at all can possibly listen all the time to a twenty minute sermon.' His fathers' discontent with any address of less than an hour or two is now a long way behind us. Some of us regret this, but we had better get used to it. We have to communicate with people as they are, and that seems to call not only for brevity over-all but for as many scene changes as possible even within that brief compass.

Then again, a television documentary needs to have not only the quality of dramatic dialogue in order to hold the interest, but also an over-all dramatic shape in order to move the viewer towards some kind of climax. Programmes rarely end with firm conclusions firmly presented as the assured outcome of the investigation, but the action has to keep moving and the plot unfolding. When the end comes, the presenter's last statement may be another question, or may be the first question re-stated in the light of the evidence submitted. There is an unspoken – or even spoken – 'over to you' addressed to the audience as to a jury which must reach its own verdict.

Not every preacher would want to end in such a way. Not every preacher should. But there is something to be said for an ending which points the congregation on to further enquiries and experiment in preference to the 'that settles that' type of climax. Every monologue communication needs the kind of wholeness which comes from showing at the end that all this has been relevant to the question which was raised at the beginning, but the question need not have been disposed of. As dialogue communication a certain element of open-endedness is appropriate, a certain readiness for further contributions to be made in ongoing discussion and experience. Pastor Robinson told the Pilgrim Fathers that 'he was very confident the Lord had more truth and light yet to break forth out of his holy Word'.

Explicit dialogue

Most actual dialogue is unplanned and informal. It is a matter of responding both relevantly and Christianly to what is being said between individuals, within groups and in larger meetings. That is how faith is communicated. Sometimes, however, Christian communicators set up formal occasions of dialogue among themselves or between themselves and others. Perhaps they should do so more often. But what is vital, it seems to me, is that such dialogues should be authentic two-way exchanges. I have known 'dialogue services' in churches which would better have been called 'stooge services'. The questions are those which the communicator wants to be asked, and the questioner puts them because he or she thinks they will be convenient rather than because they express deeply felt concerns on which the questioner genuinely seeks enlightenment. Such sessions remind one of the interviews which the leaders of autocratic states graciously grant to their journalists, having first provided them with the questions to be put – and having sometimes provided for the proper answers to be available on autocue.

There is more to be learnt from the interviewers who engage in genuine dialogue with their interviewees. Such interviewers are not limited to putting their own questions, but when they put those of other people they do it with real force and without dissembling: 'What is your answer to the people who say . . . But they might reply to that by saying . . . And what about this piece of evidence to which they might point . . . But that answer, if I may say so with respect, does not seem entirely logical/satisfactory /relevant/true because . . .'

Three comments from the very experienced Bryan Magee may be helpful to the (happily) increasing number of Christian apologists who find themselves required to ask questions, whether in dialogue services, in local radio broadcasts, in video programmes – or indeed in ordinary conversation and pastoral visiting.

An interviewer who makes a habit of agreeing questions beforehand has forfeited his independence. In some ways he becomes a kind of public relations man, helping interviewees to put themselves across in their own terms ... He becomes a tool.

... The interviewee may need the feeling that he is talking to someone sympathetic, someone who understands, before he can talk freely about intensely personal subjects, but simple questions that penetrate the mark will give him that feeling more than any formula of praise and reassurance. It is the pertinence of your questions that will convince him that you understand his situation. And if he finds that you do not pass judgement on him, neither for him nor against him, he may talk more freely to you than to almost anyone else.

... If the interviewee gives good answers he strengthens his case in direct proportion to the difficulty of my questions, and the very toughness of the interview causes him to emerge with credit. This is why able and self-confident interviewees welcome hard interviewing – have even been known to insist on it by refusing to appear unless they had a strong interviewer.[3]

As to those who *answer* the questions, the same laws of authenticity apply. They must speak for themselves. They must reveal their true feelings – including, if need be, their true feelings of uncertainty. They must be prepared to say 'I don't know' – or, more shrewdly, 'I don't know but ...' And not only must they be wholly present in what they say, they must say it in a style which is truly their own and not an affected borrowing from some model thought to provide a pattern of how interviewees *should* behave and speak. Another authority on interviewing, Sir Robin Day, has said

All politicians and public figures would be well advised to ignore any advice they may be given by the TV 'training schools' as to what television requires. They should speak on television in the style which is their own. That is what will come across if they are men of any quality.[4]

Of course, the training schools might reply that that is precisely what people *don't* do unless they have been shown that it is the right way. The union official may go on talking in a jargon specially invented for public image-building, the manager may go on sounding like the written minutes of a committee, unless each has been taught that he makes a better impression both on the general public and on those whom he represents when he speaks like the distinct individual he is. The same goes for many others who feel they are to some extent spokesmen, including those who are spokesmen of the church. They can be real spokesmen (male or female) only with the whole of themselves, not as mouthpieces of an institution, not as ventriloquists' dolls speaking with borrowed accents.

The authenticity of both question and answer need not inhibit the pre-planning of what the questions are to be *about*, and need not inhibit the answerer from getting across more of his mind than the precise form of the question may have invited. So long as the question as put is not shirked, the answer to it can be extended: 'To that I would say x, but what I think is more fundamental is y.' Certainly 'y' must be a logical extension of 'x' rather than a change of subject, but no half-decent interviewer will want an interviewee to feel afterwards that he or she was never given a chance to say what he or she was most anxious to say. John Whale – yet another who writes on interviewing after much experience of doing it – shows considerable respect for Lord Wilson's knack of getting said in an interview whatever he is determined to say. John Whale says of Lord Wilson (formerly Sir Harold and before that plain Mr – our longest serving Prime Minister of this century):

> In the experience of people who interviewed him regularly he very seldom tried to control what questions he was asked. He was content with an indication of the subjects. He knew what they would be anyway, and what he was prepared to say on each. He then simply listened for the key phrase – east of Suez, or sterling, or opinion polls – and said what he had to say. By this method even the fiercest questioners were converted into an adjunct. They became human memorandum-pads: they presented the heads of the discourse.[5]

There are, of course, limits to the lengths to which this can be taken, and some have felt that the former prime minister sometimes exceeded those limits. Bryan Magee again:

Even Harold Wilson, the greatest master of this trick of *using* the question instead of answering it, has not avoided giving quite a number of viewers the impression that he is not a straight-forward man.[6]

If such a feeling becomes widespread, the gains will be negated and the media will hit back. Milton Shulman quotes two of the cruel Harold Wilson jokes which began to be broadcast when interviewers felt they were being used as memorandum pads. His first example was

> The Wilson Credibility Test which was heard on *The Eleventh Hour* . . . 'If he strokes his chin, he is telling the truth . . . If he blinks his eyes, he is telling the truth. If his lips are moving, he is lying.'

Another was John Bird's joke on *Once More with Felix*:

> 'I was walking along a canal and saw Harold Wilson struggling in the water,' said Mr Bird. ' "Help! Help! Save me!" shouted the Prime Minister. I looked at him floundering in the canal and said to myself, "I wonder what he's really thinking," and went home.'[7]

Any authority figure is in these days subject to that kind of critical examination, and to the youngsters in a youth club the club leader and the local minister, whatever their age and however good at table tennis, are themselves authority-figures. Only a genuine openness to dialogue can disarm the resistance – but will not, it is to be hoped, put an end to the jokes.

Dramatic dialogue

Drama does not take place only on stages with characters in costume. The Bible itself contains forms of highly stylized dialogue which can only be regarded as drama, though not designed to be acted. The central chapters of Job are verse drama of the most searching kind. There is outright conflict between the position of Job and that of his friends. Although the final prose verdict is in

Job's favour, the chapters devoted to the friends' speeches are not wasted. Their error is exposed, but there is also truth in what they say. Job's insistent questioning is approved, but he has to modify his attitude. The truth is again to be sought through the tension between the participants in a very real dialogue – with God as one of the participants.

In the New Testament the difference between the synoptics and the Gospel of John is to a degree the difference between a story that is told in narrative form and a story that is told (at least in greater degree) through dramatic dialogue. Anyone who has tried to use several readers for the story of the man born blind will have found that John's way of telling it lends itself very readily to this treatment. Something might be gained if it were more often done this way in church, but as we have seen in connection with television dramatizations, it would still be important to maintain – through the context of worship or through the contribution of the Johannine narrator – the perspective of symbolism which provides the ground-plan of all Gospel stories. For instance, Jesus in the Fourth Gospel is not shown just as one who washes his disciples' feet and then speaks about it. He is described as one who does so 'knowing that the Father had given all things into his hands, and that he was come from God, and went to God' (John 13.3). The dialogue and action on the human stage have to be seen as taking place within the larger drama of which the human words and acts are the symbols.

Within that context, however, the earthly drama is itself perfectly real and human. Even in worship the members of a congregation need to feel their human kinship with the sacred characters portrayed. The dramatic form would be adopted not in order just to make the scripture more interesting but in order to get people more closely identified with the positions represented and so to feel for themselves the strain and the tension through which the truth was originally revealed. There are religious drama enthusiasts who move through every scene with their eyes focussed on infinity as if moved by some unseen force which has deprived them of all human volition and feeling. They are not really re-enacting the Gospel story. They are imposing on it an interpretation from elsewhere.

Not that there is anything wrong with dramatized interpretation as comment on or supplement to the historic drama as presented by its first interpreters. There is a valuable kind of liturgical drama which surrounds the primary action with secondary themes taken from the world of today and of the intervening centuries. The compassionate commandments of both Old and New Testaments have, for instance, been interleaved with facts and figures about the deprived people of today. Or an Old Testament story could be dramatically offset against a parallel story from later times, or a New Testament story such as that of the crucifixion dramatically punctuated by passages from the devotional classics reflecting on Christ's death. The interaction of two distinct elements provides a very proper sort of dialogue, even if the secondary element should be purely imaginative: an allegory such as *The Singer*, already mentioned, could be intercut with the Gospel story which it symbolizes, possibly to the benefit of both since the allegory would be given a historical basis and the story of the Gospels would be given a timeless and inward application.

The same desire to involve an audience in inner conflict, rather than to impart information conveniently wrapped in dramatic form for easy assimilation, is the best motive for religious drama in the fully theatrical sense. It is surprising what issues can become compelling and enlightening when personalized and characterized in this way. The number of people at present passionately interested in the nineteenth-century issues of sabbath schools and methods of ecclesiastical appointment cannot be very large, but when the television version of *Barchester Chronicles* showed such issues being discussed between Harding and Slope, thousands were locked into the debate. Nor was it without significance for them in relation to other and more immediate issues than the one debated. The likeable character was essentially right, but the unlikeable deployed the more rational arguments. To feel the tension in such a situation as that was to receive a communication not at all irrelevant to the search for sound values in our own time.

I do not mean to dismiss the value of didactic drama. In classrooms and within instructional programmes, drama as a means of communicating information is obviously valid, and it may be particularly useful when there is need for a picture of life in a different age or place from that of the spectator. But we are primarily concerned with the communication of conviction rather than of knowledge, and the kindling of conviction does seem to involve some measure of immersion in a dialogue which pulls both ways. There is a need for drama which invites a double act of identification and prompts those making it to look for some point of reconciliation beyond the ken of the characters portrayed. It is that which opens up the mind.

For the same reason, the sharp distinction between goodies and baddies, with nothing but right on one side and nothing but wrong on the other, can have a diminishing effect on the spectator. It diminishes the strain imposed by the way in which goodness and badness overlap and interact in the actual world. Having all the truth on one side of the argument is not only untrue to life but may engender an attitude *towards* life which is lacking in the openness to which truly Christian dialogue points us. People brought up on a diet of Westerns and other such simple value systems sometimes seem unable to receive bad news without looking for a wicked cause. Evidence which might be relevant can be found in many places. There is the familiar cry of the losing football club's supporter: 'We was robbed!' There is the attitude of those who insist that behind every social problem there must be some active wrong-doers – probably people in authority or people with money who are causing the difficulty for malign reasons of their own. There are even those who simplify the conflict between good and evil by thanking God for everything in their experience which is nice and blaming the devil for everything which is nasty.

It is impossible to prove that an early diet of goodies against baddies has been responsible for the subsequent oversimplifications, but 'Hunt the Baddy' could be said to be the name of the game, and there are those who play it all the time. But dualism is not the Christian answer to the co-existence of good and evil, even for those Christians who have no doubt about the demonic force of evil. Belief in an overruling divine providence compels us to recognize that contrary forces are contained within the God-given order of things. Extend that conviction into the realm of communication and you have dialogue as a proper mode for both the discovering and the conveying of truth.

Prayer as dialogue is another valid theme, but one which will be held back for the chapter on worship.

7

Theory

Before turning again to the exclusively religious subject of worship it may be useful to take a quick look at some of the rules which have been put forward as governing effective communication, religious or non-religious. Good communication is not actually achieved by the diligent observance of rules. It depends too much on the 'personal electricity' which connects human beings with one another and which Christians know as the Holy Spirit. The Spirit of God often shows a fine disregard for the rules which human beings lay down and of the channels which they dig with a view to defining his area of operation. If a particular communication breaks the rules but is effective, so much the worse for the rules. But if (as generally seems to be the case) the communication proves less effective than it might have been, then it is worth looking at the rules to see if they reveal weaknesses which could have been avoided. Laws and diagrams of communication may not be the best starting point for framing a message, but after the event it may be useful to look back at them in order to assess strengths and weaknesses in hope of doing better next time. Christian communicators have to use the ordinary human tools of communication such as words, stories and pictures. The fact that our purpose and content are religious does not relieve us of the duty to keep those tools sharp and clean.

In any case, the laws and patterns to which communication theorists point have been discovered by observation of actual human beings, and if the Spirit of God is 'Lord of all' there should be a deep harmony between the observed laws of human communication and the Spirit's mode of operation. We have already seen how the rules which a radio talks producer might lay down are very consistent with the demands of incarnational theology (chapter three). Another set of rules of which the same could be said was put down back in 1954 by Wilbur Schramm, Dean of the Division of Communication at the University of Illinois. He defined four 'proper conditions for communication'.

1. The message must be so designed and delivered as to gain the attention of the intended receiver.

2. The message must employ signs which refer to experience common to both sender and receiver, so as to 'get the meaning across'.

3. The message must arouse personality needs in the receiver and suggest some ways to meet those needs.

4. The message must suggest a way to meet those needs which is appropriate to the group situation in which the receiver finds himself at the time when he is moved to make the desired response.[1]

The emphasis here is on the recipient of the communication. She (just as a change from 'he') has got to be alerted to the message by some signal which catches her interest. She has to be shown that she and the communicator stand on the common ground of some shared experience and some understood way of describing it. She has got to be persuaded that she *needs* to know what is being communicated, and that knowing it will make some practical difference to her. That difference or change has got to be one which is actually available to her, given all the limitations which tie us down as members of groups and societies. It is obvious that only a caring and understanding communicator will meet these requirements, and that remains true whether the communicator's caring is for her housekeeping money or for her immortal soul. 'Only connect' is the appropriate slogan, and connecting means getting in touch with the real needs and feelings of the people concerned – getting in touch with them, what is more, from within a shared experience of them. And a real shared experience at that, not a pretended one. Fr John C. Kelly said: 'Here most of us fail often. We presume a "we-ness" that does not exist.'[2]

As evidence of the harmony between secular and religious wisdom on this subject it is interesting to turn to four other rules. They were arrived at by quite a different route but are strikingly similar to those of Wilbur Schramm. Charles Kraft made a study of the communication methods of Jesus as described in the Gospels. He came up with four principles which could almost be described as a summary of the communication theory to which Jesus worked.

1. For information to be conveyed accurately both the giver and the receiver of the information must operate within the same frame of reference.

2. Within a frame of reference, the greater the predictability of allowable segments of the message, the smaller the impact of that message and, conversely, the lower the predictability the greater the impact of the message.

3. The greater the specificity of the form in which the material is presented, the greater the impact.

4. Something discovered by the receptor of the message has greater impact than something presented in predigested, generalized form by the communicator.[3]

Since the teaching of Jesus was so fresh and unexpected, both in form and content, it may come as a surprise to learn that he made a point of working within the same frame of reference as those to whom he spoke (rule one). Yet clearly he did. The sower and the fisherman, the housewife and the neighbour, were not decorative additions to a teaching given in the form of propositions or concepts. The behaviour of such human beings provided the very stuff out of which the messages were made and through which they were communicated. It was by looking more closely at known behaviour that people were led to see what they had never before perceived. The frame of reference was common to speaker and hearer alike, though it took the incarnation to make that possible.

Certainly there were surprises in the things said and the stories told (rule two). The behaviour of the farmer who paid all his workers equal wages regardless of their hours of work shocked not only the characters in the story, but its hearers too. The predictable nature of so much conventional communication is in strong contrast to the New Testament model. So too are the 'predigested, generalized' conclusions earnestly pressed on us. Jesus's way of teaching in parables would seem dangerously open-ended to many today, but it made people search for the truth themselves and therefore made them value it the more highly when they found it (rule four). Once found, the truth might be of universal application, but it was through a particular and specific instance that it was to be discovered (rule three).

A concern for the personal development of those at the receiving end of communication is certainly warranted by the methods of Jesus. It is also relevant to the framing of a message which touches the felt needs of those to whom it is addressed. A. H. Maslow gives a psychological account of the needs which people feel, and suggests that each of the lower ones must be to some extent satisfied before the next above comes fully into play. In ascending order they are (according to one summary):

1. Physiological

2. Safety

3. Belongingness and love

4. Esteem

5. Self-actualization[4]

Christian missionaries long ago accepted that the physiological need for food has to be met and some measure of release from the fear of imminent death provided before higher things can be offered to an unconverted community. Yet some communicators still seem to hanker after a social order which is in some respects palpably inadequate rather than one which provides a large measure of security. Dissatisfaction at the material level is assumed to encourage aspiration at the spiritual level. This, apparently, is psychologically incorrect. Some assurance of survival at an acceptable standard of living opens rather than closes the way to other concerns.

There are also religious communicators who make a point of keeping fear alive. The old-time preachers did it by vivid descriptions of hell fire and torment. Their successors may hold out the threat of nuclear warfare or of psychological disintegration. Either way it is possible (as some non-Christian groups and organizations have also demonstrated) to generate so much anxiety that any simple formula of release (whether the repetition of a mantra or the act of coming forward in a meeting) can set free a surge of emotions which seem a guarantee of conversion.

But love casts out fear, as the first epistle of John assures us. The Christian communicator has to call his hearers beyond anxiety to love, esteem and self-actualization within the experience of Christian freedom. A state of dependence, whether physical or emotional, is to be transcended, and there is at every stage a felt need to move on to some deeper satisfaction and richer experience than has yet been had. 'Come up higher', says the Christian message. But it is less likely to be responded to effectively if it is delivered by someone who insists on keeping alive and nagging the fears, the needs and the anxieties of a lower order of experience.

There is therefore a useful distinction to be made between a felt need and that deeper need which lurks behind it and will begin to become a felt need as the first one is assuaged. We must communicate with felt needs or nobody will bother to give us any attention, but we must at the same time reach through them and beyond them to the deeper needs which are yet to be felt. For instance, people often have a felt need which they sum up in the single word 'loneliness'. They feel lonely. They cry out for company. Whoever will speak to that need can be sure of a hearing, and whoever can meet that need is doing a good work. But behind the felt need described as loneliness there is a deeper one. People are not simply in need of company. Their deeper need is to matter to somebody. Ultimately their hunger can be satisfied only by knowing that they matter to God and are loved eternally. It should be possible to speak compassionately to the felt need of loneliness, and also to point out where company is to be had, and yet at the same time reach through to the less defined need – the need to matter, and to matter eternally.

In America I worked with a group of students who had evangelical Christian convictions but were training for jobs in the media. As an exercise we tried to plot in grid form what would be needed in a television programme to connect a particular deep need with that particular truth of the Christian faith which we believed to be the real answer to it. Our grid eventually took the form of six columns crossed by horizontal lines. On the extreme left was a column headed 'Truth' and on the extreme right one headed 'Deep need'. Next to 'Deep need' came 'Felt need'. The other column headings will be given below. The aim was to complete horizontal lines in such a way that there was an unbroken chain of links between the two outermost columns. An item in any box could provide the starting point, but it had to connect right and left until deep truth and deep need were joined. And each item had to be naturally related to the ones on either side of it.

For instance, if loneliness were the starting point, then that would go in under 'Felt need' and alongside it, under 'Deep need', would go something like 'to be assured of ultimate significance'. On the other side of 'Felt need' was 'Interests', since it would be useless to address even a strongly felt need in terms so alien that the viewer would switch off (see Schramm's rule one). But lonely people tend to be soap opera addicts. Their interest is in other people's lives. So the entry under 'Interests' would be 'other people's lives'.

At the other end of the grid under 'Truth' it is not difficult to write 'God is omnipresent and loving' as the relevant doctrinal belief, but a column alongside that required this universal truth to be expressed in a particular instance (see Kraft's rule three). In this case it might be the dramatic moment when Jesus says to his disciples, 'You will leave me alone; and yet I am not alone' (John 16.32).

One column remains to be filled in. On one side of it is the biblical text, on the other side is the interest in other people's lives. Something is needed to join the incarnate truth with the known interests so as to reach through to the felt need and beyond that to the deep need. This is where the programme form has to be put down. In this example it would be sensible to put 'stories'. To connect with the column on the right they would have to be stories about real people, to connect with the columns on the left they would have to be stories about people who had tasted something of the truth in the text – hermits, perhaps, or prisoners of conscience, people who have been isolated but not alone. Since this column provides all the actual stuff of a programme it might seem that the rest were redundant, but in practice programme content often develops in such a way as to obliterate the programme's purpose. To work with a visible reminder of the larger communication strategy might make a significant difference to what stories were told and *how* they were told. As we have seen, the impact of a story and the values it communicates cannot be taken for granted. All programme content needs to be scrutinized in terms of fitness for purpose and not just fitness for medium or availability.

The scheme can be expressed vertically rather than in columns, and with no reference to any particular medium of communication. It comes out something like this – but remember that the numbers are deceptive, since the starting point can be anywhere along the line.

1. **Doctrinal truth**
   God is omnipresent and loving

2. **Specifically expressed**
   'You will leave me alone; and yet I am not alone'

3. **Communication form**
   Stories of solitaries

4. **Interests to be contacted**
   Other people's lives

5. **Felt need to be addressed**

Loneliness

6. **Deep need to be reached**

To be assured of ultimate significance

The American students demonstrated a talent for working outwards from a variety of starting points and so producing a line of communication which was at least logical, though fleshing it out would never be easy. It was even possible to start at 3, which was the last item to be put down in the exercise above. For instance, I once had some fascinating film made by accompanying a group of blind people who (with sighted assistance) were climbing Coniston Old Man in the Lake District. Their enraptured comments on the view they could not see were very moving, sensing it as they did through air and sound. One blind climber said that walking a fell was like feeling a piece of sculpture. 'You explore its shape with your feet', he said. Starting with such material, it should not be impossible to work outwards towards viewers' needs and interests on the one side, and on the other side towards the ultimate truth reflected in the blind fell walkers' experience. 'What is that saying to whom?' is a natural question to ask when confronted with such material. It should not lead to the appending of a moral, but it could lead to a way of reporting the event which released its true significance – true and religious significance – for sighted people.

I am not suggesting that a Christian communicator should sit down with some such diagram as this and plot the outline of his or her communication on it before getting down to details. (Though when I brought the grid pattern back to England some ordinands did work out perfectly respectable sermon outlines on it.) Probably it is one of those models to be used in criticism and assessment after a communication has been prepared or given rather than in advance. Was there enough material meeting the known interests of the recipients? Did the form of presentation connect with both those interests and the truth to be communicated? Were felt needs ministered to and deeper ones aroused?

Such questions are worth asking, no matter what device is used to prompt them.

It is interesting too that they are questions which touch simultaneously both on content and on presentation. The message has always to find a medium which matches it and which also matches the needs and interests of the recipient. Theology and style, doctrine and technology, religion and culture are all woven together inextricably.

John Macquarrie uses another diagram which illustrates this connectedness. He draws what might be called a triad – three lines converging on a single point. At the end of one line is A, a person who says something. At the end of another is B, a person to whom something is said. At the end of the third line is S, the matter about which something is said. At the point where the three lines converge is L, what is actually said.[5]

Two things about this pattern I find particularly helpful. One is that L stands in exactly the same relationship to all three other factors. It has to match the subject, it has to match the hearer, it has to match the speaker. It cannot be a form of expression private to any one of them – or even any two of them. The speaker must be personally at home in it (not 'talking down'), the hearer must recognize it as his own native tongue (spiritually if not linguistically) and yet it must be an adequate vehicle of the matter to be said. L must be a flexible instrument.

The other point which it is good to note is that a three-way relationship is involved. The speaker does not clutch the hearer to himself in eyeball to eyeball confrontation. He says, 'Look at this.' His posture is that of someone who stands beside the listener in order to share the view. And as a mental stance that is probably the best one to adopt whatever the medium.

But it is important to get the medium right and to use each channel of communication for the purpose it serves best. At Nairobi in Kenya is a centre for the study of Christian communication called *Daystar*. Its students come from many parts of Africa and many of them want to work in broadcasting. Its founder, an American evangelical called Donald Smith, has been forced to study the limitations as well as the possibilities of the electronic media. He summarizes his findings in this way:

Helping people make spiritually important decisions is the primary purpose of Christian communication efforts.

Six states have been identified in decision-making:

1. awareness

2. interest

3. evaluation

4. decision

5. implementation

6. readjustment.

At some points in the decision process the mass media are very important, and at other points the person-to-person contact is crucial. To say that either the mass media or personal contact is most important is not reasonable. Both are important, provided both are used in appropriate ways.

The first two steps, awareness and interest, are primarily achieved through the mass media. The steps of evaluation and actual decision primarily occur in personal relationships in the one-to-one or small-group situations. The steps of implementation and readjustment occur both through the use of the public media and personal relationships.[6]

There is a lot to be said for working on this basis, though it may be drawing too clear a line both between the various phases of Christian development and also between the roles of different media (if we continue to regard personal contact as a medium just as much as the electronic forms are). It does make clear that there are many different jobs to be done in religious communication. There is pre-evangelism and there is post-evangelism as well as evangelism itself, and it is probably right that the electronic media are at their best in 1, 2, 5 and 6 above. To make people aware of what the Christian option *is* may once have been unnecessary, but that is certainly not the case today. To interest them in it, to demonstrate its implications, to show it as a way of life – these are all necessary parts of the process, and all of them are tasks which the broadcasting media are well-equipped to undertake. The communicator who sets himself the same task and uses the same material whatever situation he is in is one who needs to take more seriously the distinctive role of each medium.

He also needs to take seriously the characteristics of the particular culture he is addressing. Christianity is the same in Kenya as in Kansas, but if the message is expressed in the same way in both places it should be looked at critically. Crossing from one culture to another is not just a matter of learning the language. The message will have to be adapted to the thinking patterns and behaviour patterns of each culture if it is to meet the requirements of Schramm's rules one and four. This means that satellite television with its ability to transmit programmes direct to all parts of the world needs to be approached with caution as well as with hope. Eager as they are to communicate their faith, Christians will not want to take a lead in swamping local cultures under a flood of programmes engendered within the cultures of the affluent West.

A study of *Broadcasting in the Third World* was produced in 1978 by Ilihu Katz and George Wedell. Its introduction summed up the situation as it had already developed.

> The broadcasting media (and particularly television) in the developing countries are in general purveying a homogenized brand of popular culture, either copied or borrowed from broadcasting in the West. This uniformity may well advance the process of modernization insofar as national sharing of images is concerned. It may also induce a standardized range of economic demands that may encourage mass-production techniques, but at the same time it is certainly destructive of indigenous political and cultural self-expression.[7]

Part of the response to this situation must be from within the electronic media themselves, and this will be touched on in a final chapter in which I propose to allow myself to concentrate on just those media. At this stage, while we are still concerned with communication principles and with their application to a whole range of communication channels, the point to be made is that communication theorists as much as Christian moralists insist on a deep respect for the person communicated with. That person's personhood must be reverenced, that person's culture must be entered into, that person's social context allowed for. Communication skills do not enable us to package messages for easy distribution in all markets. Christian communication must be inter-personal communication.

8

Worship

A good deal has already been said about sermons, stories and pictures in church services, and therefore something has been said about worship. But worship is too large an experience to be confined to services. In fact, if non-worshippers are to become worshippers it is doubtful whether the process will start in church. For many people the gap between themselves and the life of the institutional church is too wide to be easily bridged. The forms of worship used in services embody cultural patterns and words which are quite foreign to much of the population. The experience which first moves them to a sense of wonder and awe, to a sense of the holy, may have to be located outside of church premises. A more primitive, atavistic sense of the numinous may first have to be aroused. The experiences to arouse it may have to be found not in liturgy but in the life of the world, or of the community, or of the home. The religious communicator may have to lead people back to the very roots of worship and to nourish its growth in a variety of experiences before formal, Christian worship can make much sense or be recognized as real.

It might seem sensible to delay this aspect of things and to communicate the goodness and truth of the faith without reference to its dimension of worship, but that would be to communicate something other than Christianity. In fact it would be to communicate something other than religion of any sort. I take it that every religion has three aspects: it is in part a set of beliefs about what is true, in part a way of life concerned with what is right and in part a way of responding to the transcendent. Even religions which have no supreme God have forms of meditation which could be described as worship. There is that in man which insists on going out in reverence towards the reality about us and within us, once something of its quality has been perceived. This area is as fundamental as those concerned with religious ideas or actions. In broadcasting terms we would say that it is in the nature of any religion that its communication demands talks programmes concerned with its beliefs, documentary programmes concerned with its way of life and devotional programmes concerned with its response to the transcendent.

Certainly this must be true of Christianity. The God of the Bible demands worship not because he is hungry for praise, but because it is the natural and inevitable basis of any personal relationship between creature and creator, between finite and infinite. Not to worship would be not to know God. A Christian communicator might be able to communicate and kindle the Christian faith without getting people into church, but not without drawing them into the shared experience of wonder before the mystery of being, the shared experience of worshipping the reality whose name (as Exodus tell us) is I AM.

But of all the words in Christian communication the one most likely to change its meaning on the way from speaker to hearer is the word 'God'. Those who deny his existence may be denying what the believer has no intention of affirming. Those who affirm his existence have (necessarily) a whole variety of inadequate images in mind, and a whole variety of feelings and attitudes towards them. The word 'God' is used as if it had a precise meaning known to all, like a commodity in the supermarket with a list of contents on the label, but it is not like that. It is a chameleon word which changes its colouration in every mind and from one experience to another. Hearers or readers of the word naturally attach their own meanings and feelings to it, assuming that the speaker or writer meant the same, but in fact the meaning sent out may be quite different from the meaning received.

The almost unlimited scope for misunderstanding is made clear to anyone who reads the correspondence sent to broadcasters. People can hear the intended words and still be miles from the intended meaning, so they respond in quite unexpected ways. A broadcaster may have delivered some quite simple sentence in which both God and suffering are mentioned. Fiercely angry letters can come back from the audience. Probably the broadcaster took the word 'God' to refer to a compassionate being who shares and transforms human suffering. The irate listeners may have taken it to refer to a supreme manager handing out afflictions for heartless or judgmental reasons of his own. To speak blandly of God and suffering was to be heard as the public relations officer of a cruel and oppressive power. Angry reactions are perfectly understandable.

I was once responsible for a television series in which we obtained the introductory material we needed by going out into the streets, into pubs and clubs and schools, asking for the co-operation of anybody and everybody. We invited them to tell us just what came immediately to mind when they heard a particular word which we would not disclose until the camera was running. In due course I said to each of them, 'The word is: "God".' Very few failed to respond. Many immediately produced a visual image – and not all that often was it the traditional old man with a long beard. Quite often it was an image of God as a constant observer of all that goes on – 'a great eye in the sky', for instance. Equally often the mind immediately flashed back across the centuries to see God as the creator who once long ago set things in motion. Of course, many bizarre images were followed by some such phrase as 'I know he isn't like that *really*', but the immediate response to the word 'God' was frequently one that evoked no sense of reverence or love, and no sense of his immediate presence other than as a sort of super spy. Also, needless to say, the pronoun used was normally 'he'.

We found ourselves confronted with a vision of God as either remote or judgmental – and even then remote: a distant observer. People did not seem to locate God at all in the visible world before their eyes, in the relationships which mattered most to them or in the obligation (which they clearly felt) to answer my impertinent questions with candour and with truth. I was more aware of God in the answering than in the answers. The actual answers seemed to confirm what has been said already about the mental divide people erect between the real world in which they live and the fantasy world to which they relegate the idea of God.

It was not always like that. A character in Morris West's *The Clowns of God* says,

> In ancient days, when the world was full of mystery, it was easy to be a believer – in the spirits who haunted the grove, in the God who cast the thunderbolts. In this age we are all conditioned to the visual illusion. What you see is what exists.[1]

It would be wrong, of course, to try and lead people back to polytheism or pantheism, but there is the alternative of pan*en*theism: not the belief that everything is God and God everything, but the belief that everything is in God and God in everything. 'What you see' is a mirror of the invisible, a sacramental contact with the holy. In this way there does come into normal experience a dimension of mystery which is at the root of worship. In such experiences the word 'God' is far from being defined and even farther from being baptized into the Christian faith, but it begins to have some relevance to worship, and that is more than can be said of a state of mind in which the world before us is cut off from a God above us.

So to communicate transcendence we need to look at the actual world – and get others to look at the actual world – as something to be contemplated with wonder. And 'he that wonders shall reign', as Jesus is made to say in the Oxyrynchus Papyrus.

In the terms set by twentieth-century urban civilization many of us were taught to look at things in this light by Michel Quoist. His *Prayers of Life* was published in English in 1963 and became a strong influence in this country as soon as the prayers were broadcast in one of the early morning religious slots. Subsequently scores of books have appeared full of prayers in which daily experiences are made the vehicle of dialogue with God, and it is in the nature of the exercise that the material will date rapidly and need replacing. Quoist's introductions to his prayers remain, however, a valid statement of the guiding principle.

> If we knew how to look at life through God's eyes, we should see it as innumerable tokens of the love of the Creator seeking the love of his creatures. The Father has put us into the world,

not to walk through it with lowered eyes, but to search for him through things, events, people. Everything must reveal God to us . . .

    If we knew how to listen to God, if we knew how to look around us, our whole life would become prayer.[2]

Neville Cryer's biography of Michel Quoist[3] makes it clear that his ability to communicate a sense of the transcendent in the familiar was the fruit of a deliberate discipline of Christian devotion. Soon after his ordination as a Roman Catholic priest, Quoist found himself living in a sixth floor Paris flat with two other men who were also recently ordained and also pursuing further studies in sociology. They fulfilled their obligations to the regular daily offices and masses, but felt the need for spiritual exercises less detached from the world in which and about which they were studying. So they developed forms of worship which were integrated with the world about them. They would pray at their window looking over the streets of south Paris and taking into their wrestling with God all that they could see before them. Or they would pray over the open newspaper and engage God in a dialogue which had current events as its medium of communication with him. Or they would take a biblical text, study its meaning in the usual way, then take it with them on the metro, or to the shops, or into lectures, and would try to use the truth in that text as the key to unlock the meaning of every experience and every conversation that day.

    Such early disciplines as these made it possible for Quoist later, as a parish priest in Le Havre, to communicate to his young Christian workers a sense of God's being immediately present in their daily experience, and present as one to be adored.

    The communicator's task, however, is not necessarily to provide words for others to use in this way. Words may not actually be involved at all. Quoist himself says 'At first we communicate with God through words which may be dispensed with later on . . . However, the silent prayer which has moved beyond words must always spring from everyday life, for everyday life is the raw material of prayer.'[4] We have perhaps been over-loquacious in our praying and have therefore made it an activity for word-spinners rather than for the inarticulate majority. Prayer does need to be focussed and for that words can be a help, but it is possible to focus on a particular object, or event, or biblical text and to send out towards it a sort of wordless yearning for the divine reality and truth behind it. God's contribution to the dialogue would then be experienced as a growing understanding of the truth and significance of what is before us.

Just recently a Jewish rabbi broadcast a very racy account of the dialogue between himself and God on the subject of two thousand pounds which he had lost. I never believed, nor was asked to believe, that his conversation with God actually took the verbal form in which he described it. All the same, I was entirely convinced that the dialogue had been real and that God's contribution to the conversation had consisted of the thoughts which the rabbi now expressed in his own words on God's behalf. A silent exchange had taken place through the focus of an unhappy experience. No helper from outside the situation could have advised the rabbi what to say or what answer to expect. The best help a communicator could have given him would have been to encourage him to do what he did: look at the experience honestly and be open to whatever truth was conveyed to him through it. (And by the way, it was not the obvious moral you might expect!)

I remember being told that when Dr Sangster was at Westminster he used to say to himself about everything that happened, 'Now what is this saying to me?' Fellow preachers will know that there are both right and wrong ways of putting this question. It is possible for the question to mean, 'How can I *use* this? How can I deploy it as evidence for this or that point that I am going to make?' That is the wrong way because it means imposing a preconceived meaning on experience. No real listening is involved. It is a one-sided dialogue, which is about as possible and effective as one-handed clapping. On the other hand, 'What is this saying to me?' could be (and doubtless was) a genuine question, pressed with real heart-searching and with a mind open to receive the unexpected in God's reply. Such methods are not only necessary for the Christian communicator before he communicates, they are the very methods he needs to pass on to others if their innate but suppressed capacity for worship is to be brought to life through daily experience.

Many men and women across the centuries have displayed the gifts which my generation found in Michel Quoist, and some have told of the personal experience out of which came their power to communicate the sense of a living Presence in daily life. Brother Lawrence, for instance, gave classic expression to it when he said:

> The time of business does not, with me, differ from the time of prayer, and in the noise and clatter of my kitchen, while several persons are at the same time calling out for different things, I possess God in as great tranquillity as if I were on my knees at the Blessed Sacrament.[5]

This is the more remarkable when it is realized that he did not *want* to be in the kitchen, though he spent thirty years there. He did not choose that job. It was probably allotted to him because he had been a domestic servant before joining his Order. He did not even suit the job, because it caused him severe pain in the area of an old wound inflicted in his days of soldiering. He was able to draw the kitchen job into his experience of God only because he had learned to see everything as an experience of God and had begun the practice of the presence of God in his days as a footman. His own conversion as a youth had come about as a result of looking at a bare branch in winter and contemplating what it would be like in the spring and summer. The sense of God mysteriously and beautifully at work never left him, though he knew many years of doubting his own salvation. These experiences made him, in spite of being assigned to the kitchen, a great communicator of the transcendent and one to whom people constantly came for help with the spiritual life.

The same could be said about Traherne, already quoted more than once. For him the discipline of Christian devotion was a matter of recovering with great pain and difficulty a vision of the-world-in-God which had been natural to him as a child. Having recovered that vision he did what many would think a very twentieth-century thing to do: wrote a great *Thanksgiving for the Body*.

Even Augustine of Hippo is an example. He is certainly aware of the otherness of the God he addresses in his *Confessions*.

> What do I love when I love you? Not the beauty of the body nor the glory of time, not the brightness of light shining so friendly to the eye, not the sweet and various melodies of singing, not the fragrance of flowers and unguents and spices, not manna and honey, not limbs welcome to the embraces of the flesh: it is not these that I love when I love my God.

Yet he does find the experiences of the flesh to be analogies of the worshipper's relationship to God.

> And yet I do love a kind of light, melody, fragrance, food, embracement when I love my God; for He is the light, the melody, the fragrance, the food, the embracement of my inner self – there where is a brilliance that space cannot contain, a sound that time cannot carry away, a perfume that no breeze disperses, a taste undiminished by eating, a clinging together that no satiety will sunder. This is what I love when I love my God.[6]

Augustine knew only too well that the carnal experience can distort and conceal the divine original reflected in it, but if such experiences did not in themselves possess an affinity with the spiritual realities of which he made them speak, it is doubtful whether he could have used them to speak of God at all. The intrinsic connection has to be there. Without it the words would be false, and without words coined in the mint of bodily experience we would have no language at all in which to speak of God. The communicator has only the language of this earth in which to reflect the sublime light, and the recipient of the communication has only the experiences of this earth in which to see that light for himself or herself. It is then that he or she 'wonders and reigns'.

The New Testament itself speaks of a Christ in whom 'all things hold together' and who has ascended 'in order to fill the whole universe' (Col. 1.17 and Eph. 4.10, NIV). The apostles were, however, in one respect in a different position from ours. Wherever they went and whoever they addressed they were speaking, I take it, to people who were already worshippers. Some were Jews, with that wonderful awareness of God's being both transcendent and imminent: 'For thus saith the high and lofty One that inhabiteth eternity, whose name is Holy; I dwell in the high and holy place, with him also that is of a contrite and humble spirit' (Isa. 57.15). Others were adherents of mystery religions seeking fellowship with the divine through sacred meals and rituals. Even in sophisticated Athens Paul could point to both altars and poets expressing a sense of the holy mystery pervading the world of men. *What* Paul believed about God differed greatly from what most believed about him, but they met on the common ground of a shared relationship to unseen power.

With us it is almost the other way round. Pollsters report that most people believe there is a God and it might be possible to identify some shared beliefs about him. What is lacking is a sense of his presence. Many people, whatever their beliefs, are in practice non-worshippers during most of their lives, never alive to the holy mystery about them, never aware of awe and wonder within them. It is that nerve that the Christian communicator must touch, and touching it may well demand a communication more directly related to natural human experience than is the liturgy of a church service. We must attend to the religious interpretation of all experience, even if it involves giving less attention to distinctively religious experience as a thing apart.

Fortunately (but not by chance) the moments when people are most likely to be aware of the transcendent in the natural course of things are the moments when they are still most likely to invite religious intervention and even to suggest coming to church. 'Hatchings, matchings and despatchings' sounds like a derisive summary of the church's business, but the services for infant baptism, for marriage and for the burial of the dead do correspond to the three experiences in life which reduce to paper thinness the barrier between the immediate and the transcendent.

However laughable it may seem to others, and however tangled with an over-familiar attitude to sex, the time when people fall in love with each other is still a time when they are aware of mystery. The couple are drawn out of their individual isolation and in the new experience of living in and for another are made aware of the unfathomable interconnectedness of human life. Often they greet the discovery with wonder as well as with delight. It is easy to say that they want a church wedding because it offers the best setting in which to show off, but often there is also a dim awareness that something holy is involved. To speak to that awareness and to quicken it is a task the Christian communicator must learn to perform while making all the practical arrangements about where to stand and when to kneel and what to sing. The liturgical drama of a wedding service is powerful in itself, but it needs to be made a symbol of the actual experience of the participants.

So also with the birth of a child. The appearance of a new human being with all the human potential for joy and sorrow, for love and hate, is an experience which moves many who are constantly and professionally involved in the maternity services. Still more the parent of a new-born child, seeing this little thing which may grow to write poetry or to make war, is frequently jolted out of knowing it all into an awareness of mysterious purposes at work. The most rationalist of parents can feel a desire for someone to give thanks to, a desire for something to be done which will dramatize and symbolize their aspiration. Whatever the church rule book may say about the conditions to be imposed for infant baptism or for infant dedication it is necessary for the Christian communicator to enter into that parental experience and interpret it.

Just as birth signals the dimension of mystery in life, so does death. People can be very commonsensical about the disposal of dead bodies, but still the going away of a human personality leaves them reaching beyond the ordinary boundaries of earthly life. It is not just a question of what happens after death, but what is human life anyway? What *is* this existence which leaves us so intangibly connected one with another? Why do our relationships transcend the body's mortality? Such questions are rarely framed sufficiently overtly to be answered explicitly, but they are there below the surface and must be ministered to. That we must speak to real needs and answer real questions is surely agreed, but it is not essential for those needs and questions to have been articulated in words. The communicator has to sense their presence and to meet them in ways which fit the occasion and the people concerned. The glorious affirmations of the Christian burial service may go too far too soon unless the underlying experience has been interpreted elsewhere.

The sacramental life of the universe is prior to the sacramental life of the church, but the two are deeply related. The worst thing that could happen is that people might bring into church some sense of the transcendent born of joy or sorrow, and there find it trampled on by a Christian communicator's determination to transmit a cheerful and sensible interpretation of the faith. He (if we assume the service to be conducted by a man) has in fact a dual role to play. He has to make himself clear. He has to talk sense. He has to speak of down to earth realities, and he has to explain them simply. All that on the one side. But on the other hand he has to do these things without dispelling the air of mystery.

Of course, 'mystery' in the religious sense is not connected just with ignorance. The mystery in a piece of detective fiction exists to be dispelled as the sleuth explains one clue after another. The more that is known, the less the mystery remaining. It is not like that in the least when Wesley sings ''Tis mystery all'. To see crucified love more clearly is to increase the mystery, not to diminish it. In this instance the more that is known the greater the mystery. The preacher's plain talking should therefore enhance and enrich the sense of wonder. He explains but does not explain away. He talks sense, but it is the sense of one for whom all facts and experiences are part of a whole which is mysterious, fearful and adorable. The hearer should be able to say 'Now I see', but that seeing should be of the kind which opens the eyes to greater wonders before which we must all stand in awe.

For this to be the case the preaching needs to be as sacramental as the eucharist is. Just as bread and wine become the effective symbols of something other than themselves, so must words. They are earthly, man-made things (as the bread and wine are) and they must point to known experiences, tell real stories, paint intelligible pictures, but experience and story and picture alike must shine with truths they reflect and which words cannot define. Words, I believe the linguists might say, must connote more than they denote. We are back to the business of the model and the qualifier, the story which is simultaneously reportage and poetry, the history which has the down to earth reality of an event together with the transcendent and emotional significance of a myth.

As always, the two sides of each metaphor, each image, each symbol must be naturally related to each other. It is not a matter of verbal devices employed to illustrate an idea, but of that dual vision which sees the truth of things – literally the truth of *things* – in their dual capacity. To describe objects as both natural and symbolic is to describe them truthfully and realistically. That is what they actually *are*.

Children often seem perfectly well aware of this hidden mystery behind the everyday (remember Traherne), and it is a clear duty of the Christian communicator to nurture their sense of wonder and to lead it up to an adult and Christian experience of worship. Unfortunately it is quite possible for our influence to be exerted in the opposite direction. Eager to be good and interesting teachers we can fall into the trap of explaining things to a point where we obliterate the symbol and give all prominence to the fact. It is possible, for example, to take Paul's 'whole armour of God' (Eph. 6.13) and to produce a tangible example of each item: a breastplate, shoes, a shield, a sword – the lot. A child can then be arrayed in these and everybody will then see what Paul was talking about. But not what he meant! The significance of his symbols can be crushed to death under the actualization of them.

Communication which is set in the context of church worship has special privileges and is subject to special demands. Its great privilege is that it is part of a corporate activity which presupposes the interaction of the immanent and the transcendent. The basis on which the congregation assembles is that something can be done with bricks and mortar, with people and with art, with words and with music, which forms a meeting place between the eternal and the temporal. Music in particular (when it is not so cheap and cheerful as to suit better the world of the commercial jingle) says that dimensions of splendour are here to be found among the people of the ordinary world. The whole activity rests on the power of symbols, whether the symbols are the elaborate ones of a highly developed liturgy or the simple one of people gathered in silence within a Friends' Meeting House – a very strong, dramatic symbol. Whoever speaks in this context has the enormous advantage of doing so within an expectation that two worlds meet here. The symbolic and sacramental significance of the word is already assumed. That is the privilege.

The special demand of the situation is precisely to maintain in speaking that dual significance which is manifestly present in music and sacraments. Words of the wrong kind can trample under foot the growing awareness of a world set in a context of eternity, a life lived always within the experience of grace. The *right* words are not unctuous ones or sentimental ones. It is not necessary to speak as if wrapt. To speak blandly and to look only on the bright side of things is not just unnecessary but positively wrong. The talking has to be about real things realistically described, with all the pains and problems attaching to them. Tone and content alike can be plainly factual. But the facts, both joyful and sad, have to be consciously and explicitly embraced within a total reality over which grace is sovereign.

At the close of the reflections of Mother Julian of Norwich there appears a series of questions and answers concerned with her own experience. In another context and another century they might be the questions of a modern congregation at the end of a sermon. The answers should fit too.

You would know our Lord's meaning in this thing? Know it well. Love was his meaning. Who showed it you? Love. What did he show you? Love. Why did he show it? For love.[7]

9

A Changing Scene: The Electronic Media

Previous chapters have been concerned with the underlying principles of religious communication and with their application to a wide range of media and of circumstances. This chapter is different. It is necessary finally to look at one group of media on their own because they occupy an area where we seem to be standing on the brink of huge changes. It all started when the transistor took over from the valve. Then came the orbiting satellite. And micro chips. And transponders. And fibre optic cables. The technology is already familiar. The vast social changes it could bring about are likely to be discovered only in the next decade or so. The process of change has already begun in small ways, but the outcome has yet to be appreciated. The electronic media are being re-created. The re-shaping of the community will follow.

Take one example. In this country we have grown used to having the air waves patrolled by kindly, anxious, responsible bodies such as the BBC and the IBA. They have frequently been criticized, but if radio or television were not to our liking we knew who was to blame and we had the address to which to write. It may have been a bit childish of us to ask Lord Reith and his successors to save us from ourselves, but he at least was in no doubt that good had come of it. He said that it was

The combination of public service motive, sense of moral obligation, assured finance, and the brute force of monopoly which enabled the BBC to make of broadcasting what no other country in the world has made of it – those four fundamentals.[1]

The concept of public service broadcasting spread from the BBC to the IBA and in varying degrees to many other countries which set up regulatory authorities. More recently some of these have found that they are losing control – not for lack of moral stamina or political will, but simply because technology is proving too much for them. In 1980 J. G. Patenaude, speaking as Secretary-General of the Canadian Radio-Television and Telecommunications Commission, said that the critical point had already been passed.

> People have been talking about it for 10 years. Then one day it's here. The regulatory agencies have been over-run by the new technology. It may be that the definition of broadcasting is no longer adequate in this day and age.[2]

In Britain we are already at the stage where the domestic television screen is occupied only part of the time by broadcast programmes. At other times it glows to the impulses of a magnetic tape in cassette form bought or hired from a local shop. What appears is sometimes very good and sometimes very nasty indeed, but it certainly has little in common with the planned and balanced output of broadcast television. Look through the pages of *Radio Times* and of *TV Times* and then go and scan the shelves of a video shop. You will find yourself in a different world.

And this is only a beginning. The 'brute force of monopoly' (now shared between BBC and IBA) is eventually going to be challenged from above the earth by satellites transmitting directly to people's homes and from beneath the ground by cables which emerge from fibre optical distribution points to feed into those homes a whole variety of new programmes and services. In principle the family at the receiving end will be able to talk back through the cable system so that television becomes at last (in the new jargon) 'interactive'. Experiments suggest, however, that the available answers will not extend too far beyond 'Yes', 'No' and 'Please send groceries and charge to my account'. Variation on these and similar themes will doubtless be numerous but even then are likely to fall short of truly human dialogue.

But the new technology will not only face the communicator with a new kind of society and a new state of mind to be addressed, it has already put within reach a whole new range of facilities for delivering the message. The 'mass media' have long seemed huge and inaccessible. They deployed resources the rest of us could never command and rarely have access to. The electronic media communicated through sounds we could not make and pictures we could not paint. No longer. Concerned communicators could hardly be said to have woken up to it yet, but the truth is that the electronic media are no longer necessarily or exclusively mass media. The implications are enormous. Radio sound and electronic picture can now be designed to communicate with the particular needs and interests of very small constituencies. Electronic audio-visual programmes can now be a flexible instrument in the hands of the individual communicator. They can provide to the user and to viewers the shared experience which, as we have seen, is the necessary common ground for a real meeting of those communicating and those communicated with.

It could be said to be a very promising situation but that it comes about just as the mass aspect of the electronic media is changing its character and becoming a more uncertain quantity to contend with. It is hard to say whether or not opportunities are slipping away faster than they are coming to hand. Certainly there is a war on two fronts to be fought. If the channels of communication are going to remain open to fully human use, if they are going to be available to the communication of truly personal conviction, then the new technology has got to be made socially responsible in the mass at the same time as it is made a serviceable instrument of personal communication. We have got to reckon with the impact of the new transmission methods on world-wide cultural values, and at the same time wrestle with the task of getting something worthy on to electronic tape in our own back room. The first task will be to increase understanding of what is going on.

Television awareness

It has already been argued that the influence of television is subtler than has sometimes been supposed. It works via the imagination and is received in the form of images which condition our perception of the world. Measuring the effects of political or commercial television campaigns by examining changes in voting patterns or purchasing patterns is not an adequate way of tracing the communication of values through the medium. It is not just a matter of whether we respond to the television persuaders, or even of whether we copy the behaviour of television characters. Not persuasion or imitation but perception is the area of chief concern.

Professor George Gerbner of the University of Pennsylvania, after ten years of research, is said to have concluded that those who watch a lot of television violence, far from copying the behaviour of the violent criminal tend to identify with the victim. They develop a quite excessive apprehension about the amount of violence in the real world around them. They live in an unreal world not because television feeds their fantasies about what is desirable, but because it plays on their anxieties about what is to be feared.

People everywhere need help to look at television and see deeper than the surface picture of a violent world. They need practice in detecting the implicit rather than the explicit value system – see chapter two – in every news bulletin, every documentary, every drama, every situation comedy.

Too often television viewing is treated as a trivial occupation. Reading (of no matter what trash) is regarded as intellectually superior to viewing (even of the entire Wagner *Ring*). The aloof stance of the cultural snob sometimes reveals itself in the way in which comments on television programmes are introduced: 'Of course I watch very little television but I did happen to see . . .' – or even 'My wife had it on.' It would be better if intelligent people admitted to being viewers (or became viewers) and then went on to two further steps.

First they could learn to distinguish good from bad. The programme which the intellectual 'happens to see' is rarely the best on offer. In this field, as in every other, excellence needs to be sought out and identified or it may cease to be there. The way to get high quality television is to get its quality appreciated and acknowledged.

The second step would be to engage with others in the task of reading the underlying messages unconsciously embodied in programmes. The Americans have an organization called TAT. The letters stand for Television Awareness Training, and the activity if not the terminology could well be imported. 'Television awareness' means being alive to televisual excellence and also to the perception of the good, the beautiful and the true communicated by television programmes. That process has too often been an unconscious one, noticed neither by the programme makers nor by those to whom unexamined values were communicated. As the fresh waves of electronic story-telling and image-making sweep over us we shall need a much livelier awareness of their implicit values. They are no longer going to be scrutinized all the time by our social guardians. Values will be thrown up (and thrown in) as the by-product of the commercial ideas, or the religious ideas, or the political ideas of programme makers not directly answerable to the community or to its official watchdogs. Consumers of television have to become their own watchdogs, and to watch at a deeper level than is customary. To get them to do that is to stop them from being the passive recipients of other people's perceptions and to make them instead into active participants in a dialogue about the nature of the good.

In Britain a recent Department of Education report based on the studies of fifteen teachers asked not only for more social awareness and moral leadership from the programme makers, but also that more effort should go into teaching children to exercise discrimination when viewing. Confirmation of the need will apparently be found in a forthcoming report by Cedric Cullingford of Oxford Polytechnic. Reportedly he has collected evidence from five thousand children in Cumbria, Birmingham, Manchester and Texas. Most of them show positive resistance to the programmes designed for their age groups and to all news programmes, documentary programmes and discussion programmes. They much prefer (and usually see) the more lurid of adult programmes, but do distinguish real violence (which they dislike) from fictional violence (which is 'just fun'). The fact that they choose to view a fantasy world rather than the real one will not, as we have seen, prevent the fantasy images from providing the dominant values of their real lives.

Not only more discrimination but greater awareness is needed. And not only children need to work in this field. The youth club, the house group, the pensioners' club and the clergy fraternal could all profitably get involved. Human communication is a pre-condition of Christian communication. The channels of communication have to be such that people are kept alive as full human beings capable of responding to a message with a mind, an imagination and a will stimulated rather than anaesthetized by the experience of viewing. If churches wished to regard television awareness training as a form of pre-evangelism, they would be quite justified in doing so. It would in any case be a form of service to humanity.

One of the tools for this important contribution to the communication of conviction is the video recorder. Not only does it make it possible to play samples of television programmes where and when they are wanted, but possibly also to interrupt them in a way which takes all passivity out of viewing. Play an interview or a discussion to a viewing group and try pressing the pause button between question and answer. 'What do you think X will say in answer to that? What *ought* X to say in these circumstances? What would you say privately?' Collect opinions on these questions and then release the pause to see what X actually did say. It may be hard on X who had to answer spontaneously, but this is the way to get viewers into real dialogue with him or her. In any case, why not be hard on X? X has got himself/herself on television and that is privilege enough.

It is just as illuminating to play a batch of television commercials and to discuss what assumptions about the nature of human life are being transmitted along with the plug for a product. Ask not 'What is being advertised?' but 'What in us is being appealed to?' Comical advertisements can come out well under such scrutiny, as do comedy programmes generally. I have seen people almost marching to the confessional when asked (as I reported earlier in relation to *Yes Minister*) to consider not *who* is being laughed at, but *what* is being laughed at. The laugh may seem to be on civil servants, politicians, expectant fathers, amorous youths or aged crackpots, but on closer examination the laugh is always on us. We see the jokes because they expose a catalogue of follies to be found in ourselves and in most institutions – including the church.

Along with the ability to detect values, the ability to recognize excellence will also become of increased importance as television channels multiply. Increased competition has usually meant that programmes became more alike rather than more different. When electronic communication is mass communication it is natural that the more the audience is divided up the more necessary it becomes to grab the largest possible share of it in order to make the operation profitable or justifiable. And the programmes which did the grabbing best were those which were made to a familiar formula rather than those which were the distinctive work of a producer of genius. It does not have to be like that in the future if we can use the new facilities to serve a multitude of small audiences, but it will still be true that original work of high quality will only be produced if there are known to be those in the audience who will appreciate it. Similarly, the implicit value systems on which programmes are built will only be examined at the producing end if there are known to be those at the viewing end who will detect them and debate them. More television demands more television awareness. And there is going to be more television.

Satellite television

Satellites have, of course, been used for a long time to feed programme material into network television. The new development will be DBS – direct broadcasting by satellite. In our lofts we shall install a dish aerial and then we will be in a position to feed into our television sets a whole variety of new programmes beamed down to us from a satellite which sits there in the sky above us, apparently stationary but only because it is in fact moving at just the speed at which the world spins. By international agreement each country has the right to fly such a satellite over its territory. In Britain the first two channels on our satellite have been allotted to the BBC. If the BBC carries out the plan initially proposed, an additional licence fee will be payable for the right to use the DBS aerial, and for that price you will have one channel giving you the BBC's pick of world-wide television (including repeats of some of its own programmes). On the second channel, for an additional fee, you will have privileged access to special pro-grammes – transmitted in scrambled form so that only those who pay and are issued with the necessary decoder will be able to view them. These programmes are likely to include new cinema films, special concerts, full coverage of sporting events otherwise seen only in snippets, and other such goodies. The BBC is com-mitted, however, to abstaining from the use of this channel for major national and sporting events. Other channels are to be made available to ITV.

However, there are other satellites nearby. Governments appar-ently profess to believe that the area covered by each satellite – its 'footprint' in the delightful language of the new technology – will correspond to its national boundaries. A glance at the map makes this seem highly improbable. The geographical outlines of the various countries just do not look like footprints. Suppose that (say) Luxembourg were to decide to rent channels on its satellite to commercial interests (or any other interests, for that matter) seeking audiences over large areas of Western Europe. It is hard to believe that the non-Luxembourg citizens of Western Europe would be incapable of fiddling with their dish aerials until they got the programme, should they wish to view it. Cable companies could make it unnecessary even to fiddle with the aerial – or to have one. They could feed foreign satellite stations along the cable to their subscribers.

This could add to life's rich tapestry (as it used to be possible to say without being laughed at), but it could also be the way in for types of programme hitherto regarded by many as undesirable. The electronic evangelist drawing people to himself and offering blessings in exchange for subscriptions is one of those who can afford the costs of glossy production and satellite transmission. So is the commercial advertiser. So is the maker of programmes which can run in tandem with commercial advertisements because both embody the same standard of values. There are already parts of the world where *Dallas* has arrived before literacy, where quiz shows offering fabulous consumer durables as prizes are viewed by populations short of food and housing. Satellites could become the slaves of an international cultural and value system sometimes referred to as 'Euro-schmaltz', but better described a 'Mid-Atlantic-schmaltz' since it has its roots deep in the traditions of neither Europe nor America. They could become the instruments of a view of life which is not only dubious in itself but presents as the only desirable goals objectives which are quite unobtainable by most of the world's population. The combination of limited material means and highly materialist images of success is an explosive one. Some would say that we have already seen it detonated in the inner cities, but far wider and larger explosions are possible. The BBC's determination to use satellite television as a means of distributing rather than of destroying what is distinctive about the world's cultures is an excellent beginning, but it is a small contribution to a global issue.

Cable television

The subject here is not just network television delivered by cable instead of through an aerial (an experience which many people in this country already have), but cable as a source of additional programmes (an experience which only a few people in test areas of this country have had as yet). The position of cable television – especially the legal status of cable television – may change substantially between the writing and the reading of these words, but the underlying issues will remain.

They were officially examined by a group under the chairmanship of Lord Hunt. A report with a splendid title (and an excessive price tag) rapidly appeared. The British Government was known to be in favour of rapid developments in this field, though American cable companies were closing down in rapid succession. The 'Report of the Inquiry into Cable Expansion and Broadcasting Policy' recommended that a new authority should be created and should issue franchises to would-be cable operators granting them the right to service a particular locality with cable television. It was envisaged that the service they could offer would be a substantial one: network television programmes, plus 'some interactive services of benefit to business and the consumer', and in addition a larger range of channels providing such programmes as sport, films, arts, continuous news, education (including the Open University at convenient times), children's features, hobbies, health, games and locally derived programmes whether they be community affairs, ethnic, local arts or channels providing access for local people to make their own programmes.[3]

Similar expectations (but not necessarily requirements) were expressed later in a White Paper describing Government thinking and foreshadowing legislation. Cable operators who did not live up to their promises could be disciplined by the franchising body, but would be propelled by market forces and subject to few other controls. Even before the passing of legislation to set up a regulatory authority, a limited number of licences are now being granted.

The assumption seems to be that if local communities want all this local television, and if local viewers want this wide range of artistic and educational programmes, then it will pay cable operators to provide them as an attraction to subscribers. This may be a little naive. There *is* a connection between what people want and what is profitable, but it is not a simple equation. Within the notion of 'what people want' there are two quite different notions which have to be sharply distinguished. One is 'what people want most' and the other is 'what most people want'. In the area of their keenest interests people tend to break up into a number of different and relatively small groups. One group wants Asian music, one wants news about local issues, one wants help with the work of an arts class, another wants a chance to express its faith. Serving each of these groups tends to be expensive, and what is done for one of them does not attract the subscriptions of the others. Financially more attractive is the area where their interests overlap, the common denominator of *secondary* interests – old movies, perhaps. Market forces tend naturally to move into the zone of what most people want rather than that of what they want most. And it has to be admitted that what most people want, the area of their overlapping secondary interests, is an expression of what they are in the mass rather than of what they are as individuals, or as local communities, or as distinct ethnic and cultural groups.

The real question is whether cable television is going to meet people at the level of their mass interests or at the level of their distinctive interests. The special merits of cable will be found (when its technology is fully developed) in its ability to serve a wide variety of interests – and those the interests of a particular locality. It will be capable of providing all that Lord Hunt describes, including local television programmes and 'access for local people to make their own programmes'. But there are more profitable things to do. Cable could sieze the easier option of an expanded supply of formula-built, candy floss programmes of which there is already a good supply on network television. If this led to a substantial drawing away of audiences and resources from the public service broadcasting agencies, they could suffer and the channels of visual communication could be increasingly choked with fantasy.

Of course nobody should be compelled to view the sort of programmes they do not care for, but candy floss can become an addiction. The roughage of more demanding programmes needs to be among the courses on offer. A wall-to-wall covering of soft-option programmes furnishes a room which provides no window on the world, only an escape from it.

It will be for the concerned members of local communities to insist on a cable service which rises to its possibilities instead of freewheeling down the easy road of common denominator broadcasting. It will mean stimulating local interest in what could be done, calling on local talent to be available for doing it and meeting whatever financial and technical requirements will have to be met in order to do it. It is not at all clear yet whether a typical cable operating company will have its own programme production facilities or whether it will have only the means of transmitting pre-recorded tapes. If there are production facilities they are not likely to be extensive, and if there is production staff it is not likely to be large. So there will be difficulties to be overcome before local politics can be projected from the local Town Hall, or local culture projected from the local studio, or local faith projected from the local churches, synagogues, mosques and temples.

There would seem to be two routes by which local groups could get round the difficulties: one is money, the other talent and dedication.

Money provides the easy route. Production facilities and production expertise can always be hired at a price – usually a high price. Those who have wealth as well as the will to get their views across on local cable television could probably buy themselves that privilege. They could offer the cable operator high quality tapes ready for transmission while their poorer neighbours were still standing around the door discussing on what terms they could get in. But this is not a happy prospect.

The alternative is to out-bid money with talent and with the ability to get good results from the minimum of technology. Most communities contain a lot more skill and imagination than is fully employed either in work or in leisure. Someone needs to harness it to the new means of electronic communication, and then make it available to the local community. Since the churches are (and always have been) in the business of local communication, they could be the ones to give a lead.

Technical skills will have to be developed, but imagination is likely to be even more in demand. It is no easy matter to conceive the right forms for a new means of communication. It is not a matter of simply putting on to the screen what is already going on off it. It will not do – nor is it likely to be economically or technically possible – just to let cameras show what Christians are doing in churches, what councillors are doing in Town Halls or what students are doing in classes. Nor will it do simply to talk about these things down a cable. It will be necessary to find genuinely televisual ways of communicating a real encounter with the faith of the church, the work of the students, the thinking of the councillors. If local communities – or production teams within local communities – have the ability to conceive and organize good programme material, there will be a better chance of getting it produced – either with the cable operator's own limited facilities or with others which can be got at a less than prohibitive cost.

These are future activities but it is not too soon to start developing the particular skills, the kinds of imagination and the theological insights which will be required. One area in which experience could already be gained – and which is an important sphere of activity in itself – is that of video recording.

Video

Video recorders are not limited to the replaying of television programmes which have been broadcast, nor to the playing of pre-recorded cassettes available on the market. Link the recorder to a camera and a microphone and you have the nucleus of a production unit. It will not be a poor man's television unit or a poor man's film unit. It will be a video unit, and video is a medium in itself. Its special characteristics are the flexibility which it offers at the playback stage and the close focus on need which it offers at the production stage. The small group is the natural environment in which to play back video recordings, and the distinctive interests of small groups can be directly provided for. No broadcast medium can match the way that a video recording can be precisely aimed at the special needs of a small constituency. Those who make video programmes do not have to begin by asking 'What would make good viewing and be of general interest?' They can begin by asking about the circumstances in which the production will be viewed: in a youth club, a house group or a class room? as a discussion starter or as training material? as information leading towards action or as meditation leading towards worship? And what are these particular people interested in anyway? Always the thinking can be from the end-use backwards rather than from the producer outwards.

From a church point of view the work seems to be developing in two different ways – different technically as well as in concept.

Where there are many small groups with similar needs scattered over a large area it is natural for a central body to produce what is needed and then distribute copies. The Church of Scotland is very active on these lines. It has a production unit working with U-matic recording facilities – a moderately expensive system capable of quality standards not too far below those of network television. Having produced a programme of which local churches are said to be in need (documentary, discussion starter or training programme), the finished and edited master tape is copied to a lower standard (such as VHS) which can be played on the sort of apparatus now available in most localities. There is clearly room for more work of this kind, especially in view of the fact that there are in the United Kingdom more videos per head of the population than in any other country in the world, including America and Japan.

However, there are some needs which can be met only by working on a still smaller and more economical scale. This is the second way and involves amateur production groups using the cheapest of apparatus to make something which is just adequate in terms of picture and sound quality, but which has the compensatory merit of being exactly what is required in the circumstances.

For instance, the churches of an area might be running a number of monthly house groups. It might be desirable for each group to start its discussion from the same video documentary, or to build its devotions on the same video meditation. It would certainly be desirable for such a documentary to be about the local situation and for such a meditation to link with the worship of the local churches. What is more, if a local production group is responsible, the conclusions of the first round of meetings can be fed into a second video for use in the second round of meetings a month later. The electronic media need not always be the one-way systems we have known in the past. Feed-back can be included. The result is that each group would be aware of its relationship to other groups and to the churches while retaining its individual character as a house group.

Alternatively, a local church might need a locally made recording to show to the elderly, or to the housebound, or to the deprived – one which would show what help was available in just that area. Or they might want to initiate a discussion between church families and neighbouring families by inviting both to see and talk about a video programme on what is being done in local schools for religious education, or for sex education or for education in personal relationships.

A local production unit servicing such needs would need much skill and patience, because ideally recordings made on systems such as VHS will not even be edited. Recording quality is adequate where the original is concerned but drops off sharply if editing or copying are involved. It is best, therefore, to compile the programme in its final form from the beginning, getting each shot right before going on to the next. Such methods require much pre-planning, but it can be done – and done at a cost which is within the means of a group of churches, or even of one large church.

The talent is probably more of a problem than the money. It does not take too long to master the technical apparatus of a basic video system, but in two other areas a good deal more thinking is needed.

The first of these involves learning the language of visual communication and developing the skill to use it. It is strange that (as remarked earlier) a generation brought up watching television appears to have emerged from the process with no understanding of visual grammar, no awareness that there are good ways and bad ways of stringing images together, no sensitivity as to which will be the fluent way to tell a visual story and which will be the visual equivalent of stammering and stuttering. Such skills can be acquired, but they must not be taken for granted – as any experience of viewing home movies is likely to confirm.

Yet the remaining task is an even greater one. It is the need to learn how to think theologically and yet to think in a way relevant to the medium. There are those who leave all theological judgment behind them when they start to make audio/visual programmes, and there are those whose theology is retained but compels them to make turgid, wordy programmes quite unsuited to the medium. The first tend to produce poor man's television and the second tend to use video only as an extension of the public meeting or the classroom lecture. But video, as I have said before, is its own medium. It has its own standards of excellence and offers its own kind of viewing experience. Excellence in video terms is very much connected with fitness for a precise and particular purpose. The special viewing experience which it offers is very much connected with being a part of that constituency for which the programme was purpose-built, and usually with the opportunity to respond from within a viewing group.

Video productions of this kind could also be part of the answer to the world-wide blanketing effect of Western television, whether distributed by satellite or copied by the impoverished broadcasting agencies of the Southern world. I have worked with two priests from different parts who, after training, are taking video into areas which as yet do not even have television. The portable television set and the portable video recorder will enable them to use the medium of the small screen for the communication of their own values and beliefs in the languages, images and music of the region, and to do it before either national propaganda or international schmaltz can acquire the medium for different values and an alien culture.

Developments of this kind may seem to be asking too much of a Christian community already stretched to pay its bills, maintain its services and repair its buildings. It probably does mean recruiting a new generation of church workers with very different images of what church work can be. That they can respond, given the opportunity, is evidenced by what has already been done in such fields as hospital radio and local radio broadcasting.

Local radio

Some may once have thought of local radio as just popular music played on records in response to local requests. Some may once have thought of it as just network radio miniaturized: professional production units making the programmes and calling in outsiders only as contributors who work to the producer's brief. To some extent the very large local radio units (such as the London ones) were inclined to accept the second concept. Some of the smaller ones around the country accepted the first concept – or seemed to in practice.

Increasingly, however, local radio is understood as *community* radio. Members of the community themselves play a creative role in the shaping and the making of the output. The local community speaks to itself and gets a good hearing. In many cases the churches have played a significant part in this. Often it has been done through individuals who have made a ministry out of working with the apparatus and within the brief of a local radio station, but increasingly it could be a matter of volunteer production teams using their own creative imagination and their own gear to put together quite complex programmes for offering to the station managers as expressions of local faith ready taped for transmission.

Appropriate skills have sometimes been acquired in the local broadcasting system of a university.

Certainly there are increasing opportunities for churches to integrate local broadcasting with their own work so that follow-up action is possible. Lenten listening groups linked by local radio are now common and the practice is still spreading. In a typical instance the churches of a local radio area arrange a network of groups to meet at a given time each week. Representatives of the local churches and of the radio station also arrange a series of programmes to be broadcast at that time for just that constituency. Some teaching, some questioning and discussion are normal ingredients of the programmes. The radio station then turns to other business for a time while the groups take up discussion. Later there can be a phone-in session with direct exchanges between the studio participants and members of the listening groups – with other listeners phoning in as well if they wish. The manning of the telephones is also undertaken by the churches' volunteers.

The whole exercise is an example of collaborative, community broadcasting with the maximum of active participation. In at least one area where Lenten listening groups have been in existence for some years a number of their members, once linked only by local radio, have now been on pilgrimage together to Israel. The electronic media can serve real communication leading to face to face encounter and to action in community. But only if the mass media attitude is supplemented by a determination to use the new electronics for communication on the small scale.

Or something entirely different

Of course, all the expectations described in this chapter could be falsified by a new invention or a new war. Nobody can foresee what is to come. The basic principles of communication, however, will remain valid so long as human beings live, whether in great civilizations or in deserts. It will always involve the matching of the message, the medium and the recipient of the message. It will always therefore lay on the communicator three groups of obligations.

First, understand the people with whom you are communicating. Understand them as individuals, understand them as members of a group, understand them as conditioned by the mental climate of a whole society. Identify some area of shared experience on which you can meet them and which you can interpret Christianly. Take care to describe the world in such a way that they can see its significance, to tell stories in such a way that they get the point, to use words in such a way that they mean at the receiving end more or less what they meant to you. Address the whole human being: mind, imagination and will.

Second, understand the medium through which you are contacting people. This includes the circumstances in which they are placed as well as the signals you use. Whether you are chatting casually in a supermarket, answering questions in a consultation, preaching in a pulpit, broadcasting from a studio, making pictures on location – whatever it is, shape the communication to the requirements of that particular situation. Don't try to get away with a hand-me-down, all-purpose message.

Finally, seek among the treasures of the gospel for that truth which meets just these requirements – that is, the one that is most relevant to the real needs of the hearer and best fitted to the means of communication available. Don't let the packaging obscure the content.

This may seem an elaborate and unnecessary scaffolding of rules to erect around the simple and joyful business of declaring one's faith. Certainly it cannot be regarded as *more* than scaffolding. The actual building work has to be done within it, every brick laid in faith and with delight. And many of the bricks will consist of actions rather than words.

But there is more to communicating conviction than just declaring one's faith. What is required of us is more than self-expression, and more than the conveying of information. Nor is it just a matter of taking traditional statements and turning them into modern English. Nor again is it a matter of taking past experiences – not even biblical ones – and getting people today to re-live them. Communicating Christian conviction means addressing people in such a way that they meet a living God and receive from him a word which is truly his and yet uniquely their own.

Their experience will be parallel to that of their predecessors in the faith, because it is a faith grounded in history and incarnation. But it will not be a duplicate of earlier faith nor a mere continuation of it. It will be a faith received and experienced in terms defined by the times we live in – just as Jeremiah's was, or Paul's. Those to whom Christian conviction is communicated will receive from an unchanging God a message which meets them where they are and demands a response from them *as* they are, inhabitants of the global village which modern communication technology has helped to create.

Notes

1. The Nature of the Task

1. John Macquarrie, *God-Talk*, SCM Press 1967, p. 74.
2. John V. Taylor, *The Go-Between God*, SCM Press 1972, p. 18.
3. G. S. Fraser, *A Short History of English Poetry*, Open Books 1981, p. 30.
4. Richard Holloway, *Let God Arise*, Mowbrays 1972, p. 49.
5. See R. T. 'Peter' Brooks, *What the Bible Says About . . .*, Mowbrays 1982.
6. Gerhard Ebeling, *Introduction to a Theological Theory of Language*, Collins 1973, p. 85.
7. Ibid., p. 159.

2. Twentieth-Century Influences

1. Joseph T. Klapper, 'What we Know about the Effects of Mass Communication', article in *Public Opinion Quarterly* No 21, 1957, reproduced in *Literary Taste, Culture and Mass Communication*, Vol 7, ed Davison, Meyersohn and Shils, Chadwyck-Healey/Somerset House 1978.
2. Clive James, *The Crystal Bucket*, Jonathan Cape 1981, p. 19.
3. T. W. Adorno quoted by George Gerbner, 'How to Look at Television', article in *The Quarterly of Film, Radio and Television* no 8, 1954; reproduced p. 36 of *Literary Taste* (op. cit. above).
4. John Naughton, 'The Ad Man's Woman', article in *The Observer*, 22 November 1981.
5. Tony Manstead and Caroline McCulloch, article in *The British Journal of Social Psychology* and reported by David Andrews in *The Guardian*, 19 November 1981.
6. Kenneth Oxford, Paper presented to the *International Fire, Security and Safety Conference*, reported in *The Guardian* 21 April 1982.
7. Quoted by Alex P. Schmid and Janny de Graaf, *Insurgent Terrorism and the Western News Media*, Sage Publications, London and Beverly Hills 1982; commented on by Conor Cruise O'Brien in *The Observer*.

8. Reproduced in Bernard Miles and J. C. Trewin, *Curtain Calls*. Lutterworth Press 1981, p. 14.

9. Peter Fiddick, 'The Sweet Sell of Soap', article in *The Guardian* reporting submission by *Institute of Communication Research*, Mexico, on 'Theoretical Framework of the Social Use of the Soap Operas' to *Fifth Annual Input Conference*, Toronto 1982.

3. Words

1. Gerhard Ebeling, *Introduction to a Theological Theory of Language*, Collins 1973, p. 177.

2. C. G. Jung, 'Symbols of Transformation' in *Collected Works Vol 5*, Routledge and Kegan Paul 1956, p. 227.

3. Ian Ramsey, 'On Understanding Mystery', article in *Chicago Theological Seminary Register* LIII no 5, May 1963; quoted by Jerry H. Gill, *Ian Ramsey: To Speak Responsibly of God*, George Allen and Unwin 1976.

4. Martyn Halsall, reporting speech by Fred Kaan in Assembly of the United Reformed Church in *The Guardian*, 26 May 1983.

5. John Stewart Collis, *The Vision of Glory: The Extraordinary Nature of the Ordinary*, Charles Knight 1972; Penguin Books 1975.

6. G. B. Caird, *The Language and Imagery of the Bible*, Duckworth 1980, pp. 17, 174.

7. John Macquarrie, *God-Talk*, SCM Press 1967, p. 196.

8. Rosemary Haughton, *The Passionate God*, Darton, Longman and Todd 1981, p. 214.

9. Sallie McFague, *Speaking in Parables: A Study in Metaphor and Theology*, Fortress Press 1975.

10. John Tinsley, 'Tell it Slant', article in *Theology*, May 1980.

11. G. B. Caird, op. cit., pp. 177f., 182.

12. Aidan Nichols, *The Art of God Incarnate*, Darton, Longman and Todd 1980, p. 84.

13. James D. Smart, *The Interpretation of Scripture*, SCM Press 1961.

14. Thomas Traherne, 'Centuries of Meditations', I, 28, included (in original spelling and punctuation) in *Thomas Traherne: Poems, Centuries and Three Thanksgivings*, Oxford University Press 1966, p. 177.

15. Paul Yates, 'Fragments' in *The Light of Experience*, BBC Publications 1977, p. 93.

16. Kahlil Gibran, *The Prophet*, Heinemann 1926; Pan Books 1980, pp. 10f. Reproduced by permission of Alfred A. Knopf, Inc. Copyright 1923 by Kahlil Gibran and renewed 1951 by Administrators C.T.A. of Kahlil Gibran Estate, and Mary G. Gibran.

4. Stories

1. Theodore Roszak, *The Making of a Counter Culture*, Faber 1970, pp. 121–3. Reprinted by permission of Faber and Faber Ltd.

2. Rosemary Haughton, *The Passionate God*, Darton, Longman and Todd 1981, p. 10.

3. Margaret Carey, *Myths and Legends of Africa*, Hamlyn 1970, pp. 8f. (a Hottentot story from South Africa).

4. Patrick Henry, *New Directions in New Testament Study*, SCM Press 1980, p. 267.

5. Roger Silverstone, *The Message of Television: Myth and Narrative in Contemporary Culture*, Heinemann Education Books 1981, p. 58.

6. W. M. Urban, *Humanity and Deity*, Allen and Unwin 1951.

7. Amos N. Wilder, *Jesus' Parables and the War of Myths*, SPCK 1982, p. 54.

8. Ibid., p. 71.

9. Joseph Renan quoted by Michael de la Bedoyere, *Francis*, Fontana 1976, p. 11.

10. Anthony Burgess, *Earthly Powers*, Hutchinson 1980, p. 45.

11. Anthony Burgess, *The End of the World News*, Hutchinson 1982, p. x.

12. Sallie McFague, *Speaking in Parables: A Study in Metaphor and Theology*, Fortress Press 1975, p. 78.

13. Ibid., pp. 5f.

14. Amos N. Wilder, op. cit., p. 76.

15. Ibid., p. 96.

16. Ibid., p. 74.

17. Robert Way, *The Garden of the Beloved*, Sheldon Press 1975.

18. Calvin Miller, *The Singer*, Inter-Varsity Press 1975.

19. Alasdair Heron, *A Century of Protestant Theology*, Lutterworth 1980, p. 78.

20. Rebecca West, *The Birds Fall Down*, Macmillan 1966.

5. Pictures

1. G. B. Caird, *The Language and Imagery of the Bible*, Duckworth 1980, p. 176.

2. Thomas Traherne, 'Centuries of Meditations', II, 3.

3. Charles Causley, *Collected Poems 1951–1975*, Macmillan 1975, p. 252.

4. H. Richard Niebuhr, *The Meaning of Revelation*, Macmillan 1941; quoted in Patrick Henry, *New Directions in New Testament Study*, SCM Press 1980, p. 253.

5. Samuel Palmer quoted by David Cecil, *Visionary and Dreamer*, Constable 1969, p. 29.

6. John Rothenstein (ed), *Stanley Spencer – the Man: Correspondence and Reminiscences*, Paul Elek 1979, p. 16.

7. Theodore Roszak, *Where the Wasteland Ends*, Faber 1973, pp. 346f. Reprinted by permission of Faber and Faber Ltd.

8. Charles W. Kennedy, *Early English Christian Poetry*, Oxford University Press, New York 1963, p. 94.

9. Richard Holloway, *A New Heaven*, Mowbrays 1978, pp. 66f.

10. John V. Taylor, *The Go-Between God*, SCM Press 1972, p. 238.

6. Dialogue

1. James D. Smart, *The Interpretation of Scripture*, SCM Press 1961.

2. Dennis Nineham, *The Use and Abuse of the Bible*, Macmillan 1976, pp. 258f.

3. Bryan Magee, *The Television Interviewer*, Macdonald 1966, pp. 27, 34, 35.

4. Robin Day, *Day by Day*, William Kimber 1975, p. 77.

5. John Whale, *The Half-Shut Eye*, Macmillan 1970, p. 96.

6. Bryan Magee, op. cit., p. 57.

7. Milton Shulman, *The Least Worst Television in the World*, Barrie and Jenkins 1973, pp. 126f.

7. Theory

1. Wilbur Schramm, 'Procedures and Effects of Mass Communication', article in *Mass Media and Education: The 53rd Yearbook of the National Society for the Study of Education Part 2*, ed Nelson B. Henry, University of Chicago Press 1954.

2. John C. Kelly, *A Philosophy of Communication*, The Centre for the Study of Communications and Culture, London 1981, p. 46.

3. Charles Kraft, 'The Incarnation, Cross-cultural Communication, and Communication Theory', article in *Evangelical Missions Quarterly*, Summer 1973.

4. A. H. Maslow, *Motivation and Human Behavior*, Harper and Row, New York 1970, as summarized by James F. Engel and H. Wilbert Norton in *What's Gone Wrong with the Harvest?*, Zondervan 1977, p. 70.

5. John Macquarrie, *God-Talk*, SCM Press 1967.

6. Donald K. Smith, 'Measuring the Invisible', article in *Spectrum*, Spring 1980, published by Communications Department, Wheaton College Graduate School.

7. Ilihu Katz and George Wedell, *Broadcasting in the Third World: Promise and Performance*, Macmillan 1978, p. vii.

8. Worship

1. Morris West, *The Clowns of God*, Hodder 1981, p. 126.
2. Michel Quoist, *Prayers of Life*, Gill and Sons 1963, pp. 14, 22.
3. Neville Cryer, *Michel Quoist*, Hodder 1977.
4. Michel Quoist, op. cit., p. 22.
5. Quoted by Septimus Hebert, *The Life of Brother Lawrence*, Skeffington and Son Ltd 1919.
6. Rex Warner (translator), *The Confessions of St Augustine*, Mentor-Omega Books 1963, pp. 214f.
7. Clifton Wolters (translator), *Julian of Norwich: Revelations of Divine Love*, Penguin 1966, pp. 211f.

9. A Changing Scene: The Electronic Media

1. Quoted by (among others) Anthony Smith, *The Shadow in the Cave*, Allen and Unwin 1973.
2. Quoted by Gordin E. Martin, *TV World*, June 1980, p. 22.
3. Lord Hunt of Tamworth, *Report of the Inquiry into Cable Expansion and Broadcasting Policy*, HMSO 1982, p. 3.